The Art of Piano Fingering

Traditional, Advanced, and Innovative

by Rami Bar-Niv

AndreA 1060

Dedicated with love
to the memory of my mother and first piano teacher,
Genia Bar-Niv (1918-2015)

Contents

Preface 6

Introduction 7

A Short History of Piano Fingering 11

Basics 14

    The names and numbers of the five fingers 14
    Abbreviations 14
    Fingering 14
    Marking alternative fingerings in the music 15

The Five-Finger Position 16

    Pentascales (five-note scales) 16
    Intervals 16
    Triads 18
    Suspension triads 18
    Which finger starts a passage or a phrase 18

Traditional Scale Fingerings 19

    The two groups of fingers 19
    Thumb crossing 19
    C major fingering 21
    The general rule 21
    F♯ minor and C♯ minor 25
    G♯ minor 25
    Summary of traditional scale fingerings 25
    Additional ways of remembering fingerings for some scales 26

Graduating from the Five-Finger Position 27

    Expanding the five-finger position 27
    Condensing the five-finger position 29

Chords and Arpeggios 31

Triad chords and inversions 31
Four-note triad chords – root position 35
Four-note triad chords – inversions 36
Triad arpeggios and inversions 38
7th chords and inversions 40
7th arpeggios and inversions 41
Hand position for scales and arpeggios 42

Further Traditional, Advanced, and Innovative Fingering Tools 44

Blocking 44
Patterns and sequences 52
Figuring out fingering backwards 66
Sliding 67
Changing fingers on a held note (substituting) 68
One finger on two or more keys 71
Two or more fingers together on the same key 77
The thumb supporting other fingers 80
Support by the hand 80
Same finger on different keys 81
Repeated notes with change of fingering 85
Repeated notes with no change of fingering 93
The thumb as a pivot 97
Thumb crawling 100
Skipping a finger – trills and turns 102
Crossing fingers, other than the thumb 105
Crossing and shifting between fingers 1 and 5 109
Alternative fingerings for some scales 112
Chromatic scales 120
Correlation between simultaneous fingerings in both hands 122
Redistribution of notes between the hands 129
Toccata style 136
Crossing hands and interlocking 138
Glissandos 142
Finger pedaling 146
Clusters 150
General advice about technique 152

Doubles 153

    Trills in double thirds 153
    Trills in double fourths 154
    Trills in chords 155
    Semi-double trills 157
    Scales in double thirds 159
    Chromatic scales in double thirds 176
    Scales in double fourths 177
    Chromatic scales in double fourths 178
    Scales in double fifths 179
    Chromatic scales in double fifths 180
    Scales in double sixths 181
    Chromatic scales in double sixths 182
    Scales in double octaves 182
    Chromatic scales in double octaves 185
    Octaves with an extra note inside 186

Large-Span Chords, Rolled Chords, and Leaping Grace Notes 188

Breathing 198

Playing Four Hands on One Piano 199

Conclusion 201

Acknowledgments 202

Index 203

About the Author 209

Compositions by Rami Bar-Niv 210

Also on AndreA 211

Endorsements 212

Preface

This book is devoted to the art of piano fingering and is intended for anyone who plays the piano, from children to college students, from adult amateur pianists to professional piano teachers and performing pianists. The traditional basics are covered, but the book deals mainly with advanced and innovative fingering. In addition, there are suggestions about related piano playing techniques, useful exercises, phrasing, and interpretation.

The purpose of the book is to help piano players deal with the issue of fingering the music and to teach how to use effective and efficient fingering which will both serve the music and preserve healthy hands. This book is not by any means intended to replace piano lessons with a teacher. On the contrary, teachers can also use it as reference for their own advanced playing and for teaching their students.

Piano fingering is one of the most problematic and neglected parts of piano playing technique. In our modern times there is little academic material that is dedicated to this subject and that deals with it in detail and in depth. There are various booklets and charts that show fingering only for scales and arpeggios. Scales and arpeggios are a crucial part of piano playing, but these are just basics and there are all the other aspects of fingering that need equal or greater attention.

Choosing fingering is probably one of the first things a piano player does with a new piece. Some players rely on their own fingering ideas, some consult various editions that offer different fingerings of the same piece, and some rely on their teachers for good fingering. There may be second thoughts and back and forth changing of fingering until a final decision is made, at least for a while.

This book gives the tools and teaches in a detailed way how to create good and injury-free piano fingering utilizing traditional, advanced, and innovative fingering used by the great virtuosos. The book offers music examples, pictures, and diagrams, which illustrate the explanations and enable a better comprehension of the written text.

The author, Rami Bar-Niv, is an internationally acclaimed concert pianist and the book is based on his 50 years of experience concertizing, teaching, and lecturing all over the world.

Introduction

Through years of worldwide performing, teaching, lecturing, giving master classes and workshops, and conversing with other pianists and piano teachers (in recent years also through Internet groups and forums), I have often come across problems and questions regarding piano playing techniques in general and fingering in particular.

Through all the periods of keyboard music, musicians, composers, keyboard masters, and especially pianists stressed the importance of good fingering. Carl Philipp Emanuel Bach (1714-1788) said: "It can be seen that correct employment of the fingers is inseparably related to the whole art of performance. More is lost through poor fingering than can be replaced by all conceivable artistry and good taste." Frédéric Chopin (1810-1849) remarked: "Fingering is the basis of good playing."

Nowadays too, one of the primary concerns of piano teachers is finding the best approach to teaching fingering. Educators have concluded that fingering affects all aspects of performance, such as efficiency of execution, quality of produced sound, musical expression, aiding memory, and avoiding hand injuries.

Despite this, there are few, if any, books that guide and teach us how to create good fingering. Throughout the generations, a few basic rules were handed down from teachers to students. The rest had to come from one's own intuition and experience. Only a few masters actually wrote specifically about fingering in their treatises, and when they did, it was mostly just a chapter out of many or some scattered information along with other issues. It was almost always about scales, arpeggios, and their related derivations, and not much else. Not enough attention has been given in the academic literature to this subject of utmost importance. I, therefore, decided to address this issue solely and separately from other piano playing issues.

Of course, there are many editions of music that include fingering, but not all editions, and not throughout entire pieces. Some will even have alternative fingerings, but the fingering suggestions are specific ideas of one person – the editor, not always an experienced performing pianist or a virtuoso. At the same time, one can find other fingering ideas in another edition of the same piece. The fingering given in editions may or may not be good (depending on the edition, editor, particular piece, your hand size, your technique, your preferences, etc.), but the issue remains that these editions of music do not teach you how to finger it out for yourself. They do not help you to understand how to create your own fingering, nor do they help to develop a sense for and the skill of good fingering at the piano. Furthermore, editions do not talk about the connection between fingering and piano playing technique, an important correlation that should be learned, understood, and used. Some composers even wrote their own occasional fingerings in their pieces (I am not referring here to intermediate-level educational material), but the number of such cases is negligible and there is no guarantee that the fingerings they wrote are the best choices for our modern pianos, modern piano playing techniques, and individual hands.

When I was a teenage student at the Academy of Music in Tel-Aviv, my teacher took my score of the Rachmaninov second concerto (a Russian edition with occasional fingering by Rachmaninov himself) and wrote in for me his own fingering of the entire concerto. His fingering often seemed strange, but after practicing and understanding it, it was clear that it was fingering by a great virtuoso. This teacher, Karol Klein (1908-1983), came from Poland and was a student of Ignaz Friedman (1882-1948) and Isidor Philipp (1863-1958).

My teacher at the Mannes College of Music, Nadia Reisenberg (1904-1983), used to say that although we should be able to use all ten fingers equally, since our fingers are never perfectly even and equal in ability, strength, independence, and agility, we have to use the fingering that will give us the best results. In other words, it might be good to practice towards the goal of having perfectly equal ability in each of our ten fingers; in a performance, however, the most secure way of playing is to use our best fingers and the best fingering for a particular case.

Chopin claimed that it was not possible to have all fingers even and equal in ability. Furthermore, he claimed that the fingers did not need to be similar to one another because each finger had its own special character and he wrote his music with this natural notion in mind. Even though we try to make them all even, the fact remains that they are not. Each finger is of a different length, width, power, flexibility, and agility, and the spaces and spans between them are different as well. The thumb is perpendicular to the other fingers (the nail is not facing the same direction as the other nails) and has one joint less than the other fingers, but it is almost totally independent of the palm. The fourth finger uses tendons which are linked to both the third and fifth fingers, thus making it difficult for it to operate independently. We all have a weak fourth finger; Chopin acknowledged it, admitted it, and even joked about it. He said that he had two faults: one was a long nose and the other was a weak fourth finger.

Robert Schumann (1810-1856) ruined his fourth finger by trying to over-train it. Franz Liszt (1811-1886) also agreed that the fourth and fifth fingers are the worst and, therefore, require more attention. The conclusion to be drawn is that we should work and make do with what we have and use it to the best of our advantage rather than fight it.

The subject of fingering cannot be totally independent of other piano playing aspects and facts, such as musical content, technique, and size of hands. Obviously, the choice of fingering should serve the music. Often the choice of fingering goes along with a certain piano playing technique such as vertical wrist movements, wrist ovals, forearm rotation, catching the keys, etc. Modern fingering ideas are derived from modern piano techniques, reflecting the evolution of the piano, the increased need for finger dexterity, and the virtuosic demands of challenging repertoire.

The issue of hand size brings up some questions: Is having big hands an advantage? What is the ideal size of hands for piano playing? Do fat fingers produce a "fat" tone on the piano? From my experience, it is not the size of the hands that can be an advantage, so much as the ability to stretch between the fingers. This helps in large-span chords and intervals. Anything else, other than large chords and intervals, does not necessarily benefit from having big hands and being able to stretch a lot between the fingers. As long as the hands move over the played notes, small hands can do just as well as big hands, if not better. Often, big hands might get in the way, wide fingers will not fit between the black keys, and the playing might get sloppy. Small hands, on the other hand, can be quick and agile.

As for the old notion that fat fingers produce a "fat" tone, it was like the idea that singers had to have large bodies to be able to produce great singing. According to the majority of modern piano playing techniques, which rely considerably on the weight of the hands, forearms, and arms, and not simply on the weight of the fingers themselves and the muscles responsible for moving them, we do not need fat fingers to be able to produce a good sound. If one cannot reach large chords/intervals, there are alternatives: one can roll the chord, or omit a note or two as necessary. Also, notes can often be redistributed between the two hands. Other than large chords and intervals, I generally recommend the use of small-hand fingering, which utilizes a lot of thumb crossing and pivoting. My own hand span is very large, yet I almost always choose small-hand fingering for myself.

The principles of efficient fingering at the piano should be:
1. Serving the music, i.e., helping produce the desired sound, speed, effect, phrasing, style, etc.
2. Healthy and comfortable, i.e., free of unnecessary tension which can cause hand ailments and injuries.

While this book will attempt to provide guidelines, principles, and ideas, the choice of fingering will ultimately be one's own. For young people and beginners I recommend reading and studying the book as well as making fingering decisions with help and guidance from their teachers. When dealing with basics as at the beginning of the book, many musical terms are explained. As the book progresses, the narrative assumes an understanding of musical terms, theory, and keyboard playing.

Twentieth century composers who wrote *avant-garde* music used unconventional means and techniques of playing the piano, such as playing with fists on the keys, tapping fingers or knuckles on the wooden parts, plucking or strumming the piano strings, stopping the strings for the production of overtones, and even slamming the keyboard lid. Some of the music they composed is virtually unplayable as written, or requires the use of mechanical contrivances like a wooden board and other such devices. These composers invented their own unique notational systems and they were very explicit in their explanatory introductions and comments. Their "fingerings" will not be discussed in this book, except for the most popular unconventional fingering technique used for clusters.

Pianists who for years have been using a certain fingering in a particular passage may decide one day to change to another fingering, in order to get another musical meaning, phrasing, and effect. I have experienced this many times. There is not just one "ideal fingering" for any given text, but there are certainly good choices that can be made according to the aforementioned principles. Some pianists even exercise their minds and memory by practicing with different fingerings for the same text, but these will not necessarily be the best choices of fingerings. Whenever there is a dilemma regarding a choice between what seem to be several equally good fingerings, I recommend to practice (as I do myself) all the choices and master them to perfection, after which, one can make a well-informed decision.

Arriving at good fingering can give great pleasure and satisfaction, which is in addition to the pleasure and satisfaction derived from the beauty of the music itself. It enables one to enjoy the playing and the music so much more. This may be an important motivation for the careful study of fingering presented in this book.

I use in this book the American terms for note values; here are the British equivalents:

whole note = semibreve;   half note = minim;   quarter note = crotchet; eighth note = quaver;   16th note = semiquaver;   32nd note = demisemiquaver.

A Short History of Piano Fingering

Before the 16th century there was no specific fingering method, as the keyboard instruments were very primitive. The music was written only in simple musical keys and there was almost no need to use the black keys of the instrument. That is, black keys as we know them on the modern piano; some early keyboard instruments had the colors of the keys reversed. Until the second half of the 17th century, the thumb and the little finger were hardly used in keyboard playing. They would hang loosely outside the keyboard and only the three middle fingers were used, lying flat on the keys. Playing with just the three middle fingers was the most comfortable way since the keyboard was placed much higher than on our modern pianos. It was also difficult to raise the thumb and the little finger above the keyboard, since the elbow was hanging low, rather than in a horizontal line with the hand on the keyboard as is done nowadays.

The fingers were numbered in various ways. Alessandro Scarlatti (1660-1725), the father of Domenico, gave the fingers symbols rather than numbers. The thumb was marked zero by some musicians until as late as the middle of the 18th century.

A milestone work by François Couperin (1668-1733), *L'Art de toucher le clavecin* (*The Art of Harpsichord Playing*) was published in 1716. This was his most famous book and it contained suggestions for fingerings, ornamentation, touch and other features of keyboard technique. Bach was influenced by it and adopted the fingering system that Couperin set forth for playing the harpsichord, including the use of the thumb.

Johann Sebastian Bach (1685-1750), the great innovator of the musical art, was also known as revolutionary in keyboard fingering. His innovations in the temperament of notes within the music keys, *Well Tempering*, called for expanding the playing technique. The black keys became as important as the white keys, and the thumb and little finger were raised onto the keyboard and became fully active in playing. This enabled agile playing on all the keys of the instrument, including the black ones. The thumb became very important as a pivot for changing to higher or lower hand positions on the keyboard via crossings, thus enabling the smooth playing of scales and arpeggios.

Although the thumb and the little finger were not yet used freely on the black keys, these innovations led to modern fingering. At that time and as a result of using all of the fingers on the keyboard, the fingers became somewhat curved while playing, which enabled more flexibility than the previous method of keeping them flat on the keys.

It is quite clear from the music of Jean-Philippe Rameau (1683-1764) that, like his contemporaries, he cultivated a system tending toward equal development and independence of the five fingers in both hands.

Another important innovator in the art of keyboard playing was Domenico Scarlatti (1685-1757), a contemporary of J. S. Bach. He developed virtuosity and enriched the playing technique with important tricks like crossing hands, long span arpeggios, phrases of double notes, fast repetition of notes, etc. As a result of these innovations, Scarlatti will be remembered in the history of music as the father of modern piano playing.

The sons of J. S. Bach as well as W. A. Mozart (1756-1791) and other prominent 18th century musicians and keyboardists continued to develop keyboard playing techniques and fingering ideas. J. S. Bach's son, the composer Carl Philipp Emanuel (1714-1788), is also known for his 1753 book *Versuch über die wahre Art das Clavier zu spielen* (*Essay on the true art of playing keyboard instruments*). In this book C. P. E. devotes the first chapter to fingering.

These masters of the keyboard, including Mozart in his early days, were actually renowned for being distinguished experts of the harpsichord. The first to acknowledge the special qualities of the piano was Muzio Clementi (1752-1832). He wrote the first *Sonatas* intended to be played exclusively on the piano in 1773.

The second half of the 18th century and the 19th century produced great teachers like Clementi, Johann Nepomuk Hummel (1778-1837), Carl Czerny (1791-1857), and Adolph Kullak (1823-1862), who wrote technique books and exercises for piano playing.

In the 19th century, with new technical demands presented by the rich music of Beethoven (1770-1827), Chopin (1810-1849), Liszt, and others, the art of fingering was once again raised to new heights.

For many years, the piano pedagogues preached the notion that the thumb should not be used on the black keys. Only in the time of Chopin and Liszt was this changed. In our modern times pianists do not hesitate to use the thumb on any key and in any passage.

The following example, taken from a 19th century music edition, can attest to the thumb being somewhat of an outcast, even though modern techniques in those days already fully employed the thumb. This edition still used the old finger numbering system of the index finger being finger number one, as in violin playing. Once keyboardists started using the thumb consistently, however, a new form of notation was needed. Instead of changing the finger numbering system, British editors simply added a little plus sign (+) to indicate the use of the thumb (English Fingering). The music example below shows thirteen measures from Beethoven's *Sonata No. 8 in C minor, Op. 13, Pathétique*, as published by this edition. We can see the plus marks indicating the thumb while the other fingering numbers actually indicate, according to our modern system (Continental Fingering), one number higher than written. The fingering in this edition is not by Beethoven.

It is interesting to note that Hector Berlioz (1803-1869) did not approve of marking the music score so as to instruct the player of the correct use of fingering. He claimed that the player should be given more freedom in searching and finding an independent way of fingering the passages to be played. He felt that it would be better if each player adopted an individual technical solution without having to depend on ideas of others.

By the early 20th century, all piano makers fully adopted the cast-iron frame of the piano, which was invented in the first half of the 19th century. It made it possible to produce the coveted bigger sound from the piano, and it allowed for larger concert halls. This invention resulted in a considerably heavier action for the instrument. In addition, it soon became apparent that finger technique alone was not sufficient to meet the needs of the increasingly challenging keyboard repertoire. New piano playing techniques emerged, employing more arm weight and more wrist and forearm motion. Both the new heavier keyboard action and new playing techniques required new approaches to fingering.

In our time, various fingering suggestions may be found in many music scores. Some pianists and teachers do not agree with the need to supply fingering in the score and prefer editions with no fingering suggestions or any other heavy editing for that matter. Expert pianists choose their own efficient fingering according to their knowledge, understanding, and experience.

Basics

The names and numbers of the five fingers

The thumb is finger number one.
The index finger is finger number two.
The middle finger is finger number three.
The ring finger is finger number four.
The little finger (the pinky) is finger number five.

Abbreviations

LH = Left Hand.
RH = Right Hand.
As a rule, the text in the book refers to the photo/figure/music example which follows, unless specifically stated otherwise.

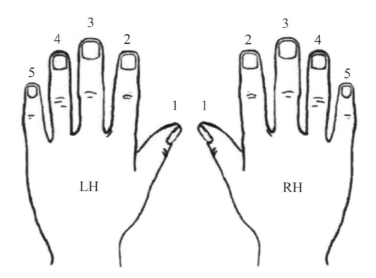

Fingering

Fingering means the assignment of fingers to notes, or in other words, which finger plays which note. Fingering is indicated in the music by the numbers of the fingers which can appear above, below, or to the sides of the notes. When we have harmonic intervals (two notes played together), or chords (three or more notes played together) in one hand, the finger numbers for the particular interval/chord are written one on top of the other, low pitch at the bottom, and high pitch at the top. This means that the RH chord fingering will be written from the bottom up starting with the thumb, and the LH chord fingering will be written from the bottom up starting with the little finger. Usually, the upper staff and the treble clef will serve the RH notes, while the lower staff and the bass clef will serve the LH notes. But either hand can play anywhere on the piano keyboard and, therefore, can have notes written for it in either staff and in either clef. Sometimes a single piano system can include three or even four staves. Sometimes the system is a single staff. When both hands play together, normally the RH will play the higher pitched notes, and the LH will play the lower pitched notes. When necessary, which hand plays what notes can be indicated either by stems up for the RH, and down for the LH (sometimes the opposite, too), or by simply marking LH for the left hand, and RH for the right hand, with or without brackets. Other languages, of course, have other abbreviations for marking the hands. Some editions mark this difference by placing one hand's fingering above the notes and the other below the notes.

Marking alternative fingerings in the music

Alternative fingering possibilities can be marked in various ways:
1. Stacked with a small line between the finger numbers.
2. In parenthesis.
3. With a horizontal line between the two fingerings.
4. One fingering above the notes, and the other fingering below the notes, with or without parenthesis.
5. The multiple fingerings stacked without any particular added marks.
6. Horizontally with a small slash between the finger numbers.

The next RH music example will show various ways of marking alternative fingerings; some are found in scores more often than others.

When figuring out fingering for yourself, it is a good idea to write down your initial fingering in the music score as well as any alternative fingerings and changes of fingerings.

The Five-Finger Position

Pentascales (five-note scales)

The most commonly used fingering for any five consecutive diatonic notes is the five consecutive fingers. This is referred to as the five-finger position. For ease of explanation, I will primarily refer to the white keys in the examples that follow. For example, on the keys C-D-E-F-G we will put the RH fingers 1-2-3-4-5, or the LH fingers 5-4-3-2-1.

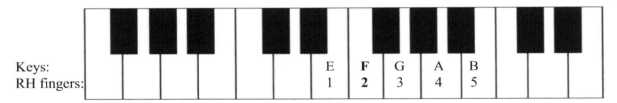

This five-finger position means that if one finger is indicated for a certain note, the rest of the fingers in the same hand are arranged accordingly on the neighboring notes. For example, RH finger 2 on F means finger 1 on E, finger 3 on G, finger 4 on A, and finger 5 on B.

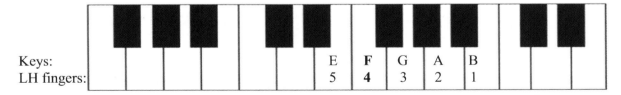

LH finger 4 on F means finger 5 on E, finger 3 on G, finger 2 on A, and finger 1 on B.

Intervals

The five-finger position also means that if we skip a white key (an interval of a third) we skip a finger too, if we skip two white keys (an interval of a fourth) we skip two fingers, and if we skip three keys (an interval of a fifth) we skip three fingers. Obviously, if we just make a step from any white key to the neighboring white key (an interval of a second) we use two neighboring fingers. Therefore, fingering the intervals of a second, a third, a fourth, and a fifth also derives from the five-finger position. For the interval of a second (a step), we will use fingers 1 and 2, or 2 and 3, or 3 and 4, or 4 and 5. This is good for any two neighboring white keys, and often also on any of the neighboring black keys within their groups.

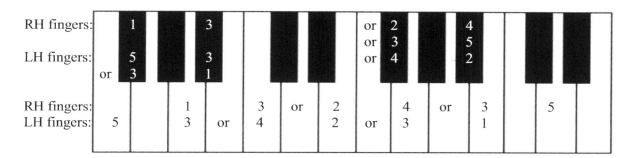

For the interval of a third (a skip), we will use fingers 1 and 3, or 2 and 4, or 3 and 5. This is good for any skip between white keys, and often also for skipping the middle black key in the group of three black keys.

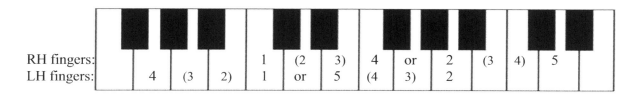

For the interval of a fourth (a step plus a skip), we will use fingers 1 and 4, or fingers 2 and 5.

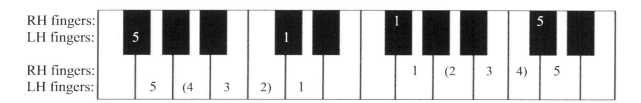

For the interval of a fifth (two skips), we will use fingers 1 and 5.

Triads

Fingering triads (three-note chords and arpeggios) in the root position also derives from the five-finger position. For example, on the notes C-E-G we will put the RH fingers 1-3-5, or the LH fingers 5-3-1.

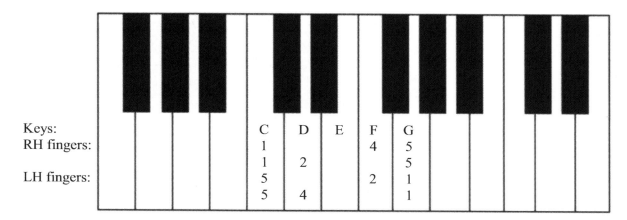

Suspension triads

The fingering of a root position three-note chord and arpeggio with the fourth or second note in the middle instead of the third note, also derives from the five-finger position. For example, on the notes C-F-G we will put the RH fingers 1-4-5, or the LH fingers 5-2-1. On the notes C-D-G we will put the RH fingers 1-2-5, or the LH fingers 5-4-1.

Keys:	C	D	E	F	G
RH fingers:	1			4	5
	1	2			5
LH fingers:	5			2	1
	5	4			1

Which finger starts a passage or a phrase

A good basic rule, absent a specific reason to do otherwise, is to start with a low numbered finger if the RH notes move upwards on the keyboard, or the LH notes move downwards on the keyboard, and to start with a high numbered finger if the RH notes move downwards on the keyboard, or the LH notes move upwards on the keyboard. Following this logical rule will ensure that we have enough fingers available to play the upcoming notes in the direction we are moving.

Traditional Scale Fingerings

The two groups of fingers

All traditional fingerings of scales are based on using two groups of consecutive fingers in a row: the group of the three fingers 1-2-3, and the group of the four fingers 1-2-3-4. Together these two groups cover seven notes, which is what we need to cover in a scale. The order of these two fingering groups depends on the keyboard topography of the scale. These two groups do not necessarily have to start from the beginning; they can start, and therefore also end, on any of the fingers in the series. The order of the fingers within the group is always kept, and one group always follows the other. The little finger is used instead of crossing the thumb for some endings in the RH, and some beginnings in the LH, but has no actual bearing on the scale fingering. Some scales do not employ the little finger at all.

Thumb crossing

The idea of using consecutive fingers on consecutive notes is kept when fingering scales. Since scales contain more than just five notes that can be covered by the five-finger position, we incorporate thumb crossing, which makes it possible to smoothly connect between the two fingering groups mentioned above, and thus reach new hand positions. When the RH ascends, and the LH descends, the thumb passes under the other fingers.

When the RH descends, and the LH ascends, the other fingers pass over the thumb.

Thumb crossing exercises: play the four notes repeatedly, every time with a different fingering out of the eight fingerings marked one on top of the other. The fingerings are effective for either hand.

Also in the next two exercises, keep on repeating the measure with each hand using the four different fingerings.

The reader is encouraged to create more thumb crossing exercises along these lines: exercises which employ larger intervals, the use of black keys, and fingerings of various scales and arpeggios. Here is just one more variation of the thumb crossing exercises, this time the thumb will be moving back and forth while another finger will be staying still. As before, the four different fingerings are effective for either hand.

C major fingering

RH ascending: 1-2-3-1-2-3-4-5. Return with the same fingering in reverse order. If we want to continue and play another ascending octave, instead of finishing on C with finger 5 we will again cross the thumb onto it so we can continue as if we are starting from the beginning of the fingering. Therefore, two octaves of the RH ascending will be fingered: 1-2-3-1-2-3-4-<u>1</u>-2-3-1-2-3-4-5. LH ascending will be fingered: 5-4-3-2-1-3-2-1. Return with the same fingering in reverse order. If we want to continue and play another ascending octave, we cross finger 4 onto D.

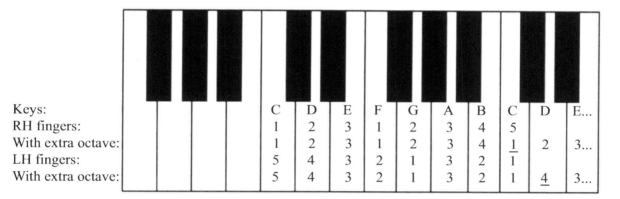

Keys:	C	D	E	F	G	A	B	C	D	E...
RH fingers:	1	2	3	1	2	3	4	5		
With extra octave:	1	2	3	1	2	3	4	<u>1</u>	2	3...
LH fingers:	5	4	3	2	1	3	2	1		
With extra octave:	5	4	3	2	1	3	2	1	<u>4</u>	3...

Playing this type of fingering hands together in contrary motion where the notes move in opposite directions is mentally more comfortable than playing it in parallel motion where the notes move in the same direction. While the motion is contrary, the fingerings of both hands are parallel, as they create symmetry by mirroring each other exactly.

The general rule

Most scales are fingered based on the inverse relationship between the way the keyboard is built and the way our hand is built. The keyboard has long white keys and short black keys. Our hand has three long fingers (fingers 2-3-4) and two short ones (the thumb and the little finger). The long fingers usually play on the black keys (the short keys), and the short fingers usually play on the white keys (the long keys). The black keys are divided into two groups: one of two black keys and the other of three black keys.

Fingers 2 and 3 usually play on the groups of two black keys.

A reminder hint could be the peace/victory sign.

Fingers 2, 3, and 4 usually play on the groups of three black keys.

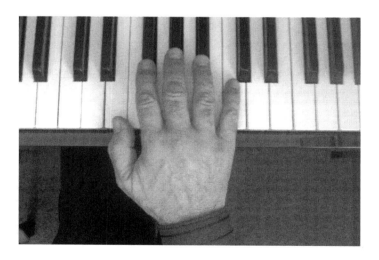

A reminder hint could be the scouts sign/salute.

Following is a figure showing the relevant fingering groups for the black keys.

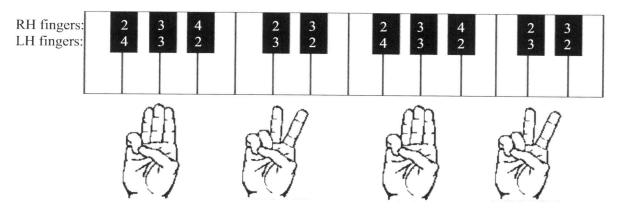

The thumb usually plays on one of the adjacent white keys B-C or E-F.

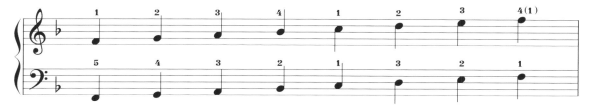

The little finger is hardly used in any scale fingering. When it is used, it appears only once in the entire scale and it plays on one of the white keys at the very bottom end of some scales in the LH, and at the very top end of some scales in the RH. Actually in the scales fingered with the "General rule" principles, the little finger is used only once per scale, only in one hand, and only in four scales as follows: B major and B minor in the RH on the very top note B; F major and F minor in the LH on the very bottom note F. Incidentally, the fingerings of these same four scales in the respective hands also fall under the category of "C major fingering".

Finger 4 is used also in place of the thumb on B at the very bottom end of the B major and B minor scales in the LH, and on F at the very top end of the F major and F minor scales in the RH.

F major scale fingering:

B major scale fingering:

These ideas are also applicable to scales which do not employ all five different black keys, i.e., when one or more of the notes that can be raised by a sharp or lowered by a flat, from a white to a black key, are kept natural. Even the fingering of the ascending RH in the C major scale, which is all white keys (1-2-3-1-2-3-4-5), can be viewed as deriving from this "General rule". In C major the white keys D and E are played with fingers 2 and 3, the same fingers that we typically use on the two black keys D♭ and E♭; the white keys G, A, and B are played with fingers 2, 3, and 4, the same fingers that we typically use on the three black keys G♭, A♭, and B♭.

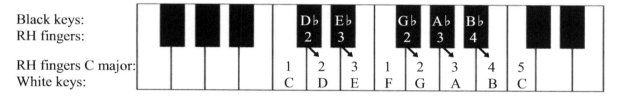

The traditional fingering for an ascending C major scale in the LH does not derive from the "General rule" as it does in the RH. If we were to use in the LH the same idea of fingering deriving from the "General rule" instead of using the "C major fingering", it would be more advanced and would produce the fingering 4-3-2-1-4-3-2-1, which is also discussed later on in "Alternative fingerings for some scales". This is the same LH fingering as in the ascending B major scale which does derive from the same "General rule" principles. C♯ and D♯, the group of two black keys in B major, are the same keys as D♭ and E♭, respectively. In C major, the keys D and E would be played with fingers 3 and 2 of the two black keys D♭ and E♭. F♯, G♯, and A♯, the group of three black keys in B major, are the same keys as G♭, A♭, and B♭. In C major, the keys G, A, and B, would be played with fingers 4, 3, and 2 of the three black keys G♭, A♭, and B♭.

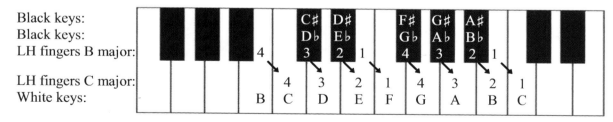

The above "General rule" is an excellent guideline not only for scales but also for piano playing in general.

F♯ minor and C♯ minor

The LH follows the "General rule". The RH could also follow the "General rule", but the traditional fingering is different. If we follow the traditional fingering, the RH fingering will be: 3-4-1-2-3-1-2-3, except for ascending melodic, which is 2-3-1-2-3-4-1-2. When returning without repeating the top note, playing the natural mode, we need to end with finger 3. We can also return not in the traditional way, playing the natural mode using the same fingering we used for the ascending melodic mode. As a matter of fact, we can use the ascending melodic fingering in both directions of the scale for all three minor modes, natural, harmonic, and melodic. When this above fingering for the melodic scale is used for C♯ minor, it follows the "General rule". F♯ minor also has another possibility for an ascending melodic RH fingering, which derives from the "General rule": 2-3-4-1-2-3-1-2. As above, returning without repeating the top note, playing the natural mode while using its traditional fingering, we need to end with finger 3. We can also return playing the natural mode using the same fingering we used for ascending the melodic mode. As a matter of fact, we can use this ascending melodic fingering in both directions of the scale for all three minor modes, natural, harmonic, and melodic.

G♯ minor

Both hands follow the "General rule". However, the LH in the harmonic and in the ascending melodic would most likely fare better with the following option: 3-2-1-4-3-2-1-3.

Summary of traditional scale fingerings

Major scales: C, G, D, A, E: "C major fingering".
Minor scales: C, G, D, A, E: "C major fingering".
Major scales: B, F, C♯/D♭, F♯/G♭: "General rule".
Minor scales: B, F, A♯/B♭, D♯/E♭, G♯/A♭: "General rule".
G♯ minor harmonic and ascending melodic recommended option for
LH: 3-2-1-4-3-2-1-3.
Major scales: B♭, E♭, A♭ RH: "General rule".
LH: 3-2-1-4-3-2-1-3.
Minor scales: F♯, C♯ RH: 3-4-1-2-3-1-2-3, except for ascending melodic, which is 2-3-1-2-3-4-1-2. When intending to return in the natural mode, without repeating the top note, while using its traditional fingering, we need to end the melodic ascent with finger 3 instead of finger 2.
LH: "General rule".

Additional ways of remembering fingerings for some scales

1. Major scales B♭, E♭, A♭, D♭ LH: start with 3, cross to 4 (3-2-1-4-3-2-1-3). It might be good to note that LH finger 4 falls on the new flat in the key signature of the scale. The new flat is also the next scale when following the order in the circle of fourths.

2. The fourth finger of each hand is used only once per octave; therefore, it is a good idea to know – for every scale and each hand – which note is the one played by the fourth finger. The scales of B major and B minor start in the LH with finger 4, thus seemingly making it appear twice in the same octave, but it is really the thumb that falls on the note B at the beginning of the scale (this is verified in the next octave), and we start with finger 4 in order to avoid additional and unnecessary crossing. For example, in the major and minor scales C, G, D, A, E, the RH fourth finger falls on the seventh degree of the scale which is the leading tone or the subtonic in natural minor. The LH fourth finger falls on the second degree of the scale. The following is a more specific example. In the G major scale the RH fourth finger falls on F♯, and the LH fourth finger falls on A.

G major scale:

All these scale-fingering ideas can be used not only for the major and minor scales but also for various other modes. A good exercise is practicing scales beginning with every note of the scale (not just the tonic) as if playing the various modes while keeping the same fingers on the same notes as when starting from the tonic. For example, in C major start with the RH second finger on D and the LH fourth finger on a lower D, play in both hands an octave or two up to D (you are actually playing the Dorian mode) and return reversing the same fingering. Then start with the RH third finger on E and the LH third finger on a lower E, play in both hands an octave or two up to E (now you are actually playing the Phrygian mode) and return reversing the same fingering. Keep going like this starting from each note of the scale, thus playing all the modes, but instead of starting each of these modes with the RH thumb and the LH little finger, you start with the fingers that fall on these starting notes when playing the C major scale with its traditional fingering.

Graduating from the Five-Finger Position

The five-finger position is the fundamental fingering idea on which everything else is based. But with the five-finger position alone we cannot get very advanced in piano playing. We now need to graduate from the five-finger position. We do that by expanding, and by condensing the position.

Expanding the five-finger position

Our fingers are flexible and can move in any direction. Spreading the fingers to widen the spaces between them enables us to reach larger spans on the keyboard. The largest space we can spread between two neighboring fingers exists between the thumb and finger 2. This makes it very easy to expand the five finger position to a sixth key by moving the thumb one key further away from the other fingers, and skipping a key.

Fingering many chords/arpeggios within the frame of the interval of a sixth derives from this. So if we want to finger the RH chord C\E\A, we will use fingers 1\2\5. If we want to finger the same chord in the LH we will use fingers 5\3\1. In both cases fingers 2, 3, 4, 5 are arranged consecutively on the keys like in the five-finger position while the thumb is moved away from the other fingers skipping one key (marked in the following figure with a zero).

Interval of a sixth between C and A:

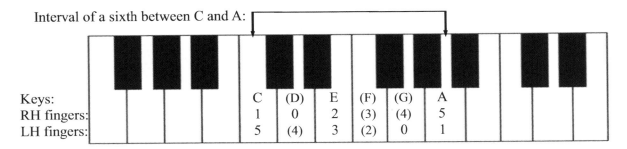

Keys:					C	(D)	E	(F)	(G)	A				
RH fingers:					1	0	2	(3)	(4)	5			
LH fingers:					5	(4)	3	(2)	0	1			

The thumb can move further from the other fingers, and skip more than one key as shown in the following photo.

If we want to play the chord A\D\G, we will use fingers 1\2\5 for the RH, and 5\2\1 for the LH. Again, fingers 2, 3, 4, 5 are arranged consecutively on the keys like in the five-finger position while the thumb is moved away from the other fingers, this time skipping two keys (marked in the following figure with zeros).

Keys:			A	(B)	(C)	D	(E)	(F)	G					
RH fingers:			1	0	0	2	(3)	(4)	5				
LH finger:			5	(4)	(3)	2	0	0	1				

As a matter of fact, every finger can move away from its neighboring finger on either side and skip a key quite comfortably. All fingerings for advanced chords and arpeggios derive from these expansions of the five-finger position.

Condensing the five-finger position

Often we need to contract the hand, and skip a finger,

or skip two fingers,

or even skip three fingers.

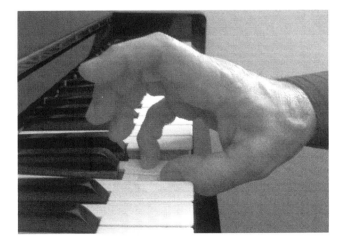

This is a very important tool of fingering. In order to play the next sequence in the RH (the fingering is written on top of the notes) we need to contract the hand when we play the key G and move the thumb from the key C to the key D. In the LH (the fingering is written under the notes) we need to contract the hand when we play the key G and move the little finger from the key C to the key D.

In order to play the next sequence in the RH (fingering is on top of the notes) we need to contract the hand when we play the key G and move the thumb all the way from the key C to the key F. In the LH (fingering is under the notes) we need to contract the hand when we play the key G and move the little finger all the way from the key C to the key F.

The following little phrase also calls for contracting the hands and skipping a finger. We have three different fingerings for each hand (the RH fingering is written on top of the notes and the LH fingering is written under the notes). Every fingering employs the tool of skipping a finger but it skips different fingers. The end result is the same, and we land the RH thumb and the LH little finger on the key D.

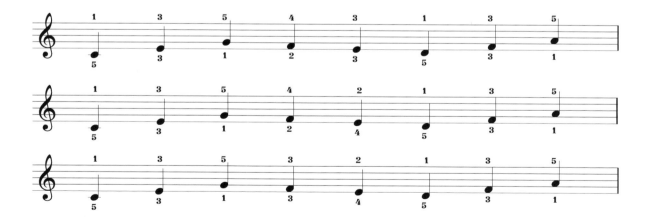

Chords and Arpeggios

Triad chords and inversions

Traditionally, and when these chords stand alone, we use fingers 1, 3, and 5 for the root position.

RH root position:

LH root position:

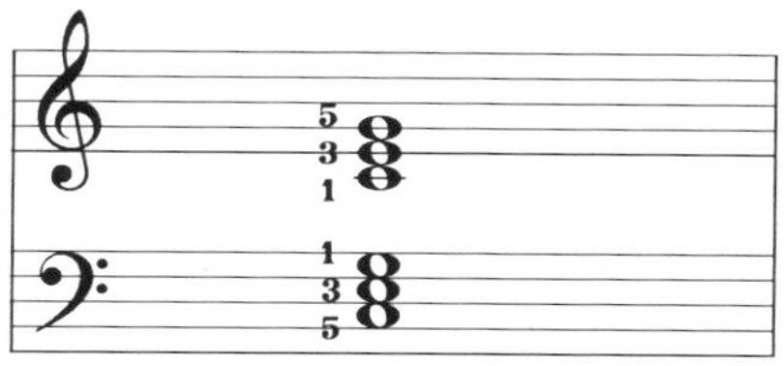

For the first inversion in the RH and the second inversion in the LH we use the second finger in the middle.

RH first inversion:

LH second inversion:

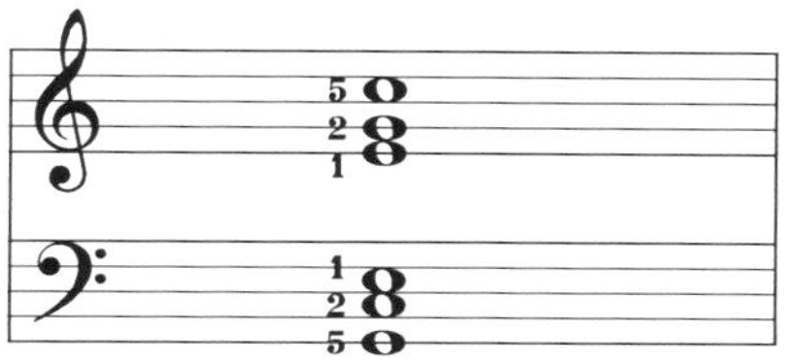

For the second inversion in the RH and the first inversion in the LH we use the third finger in the middle.

RH second inversion:

LH first inversion:

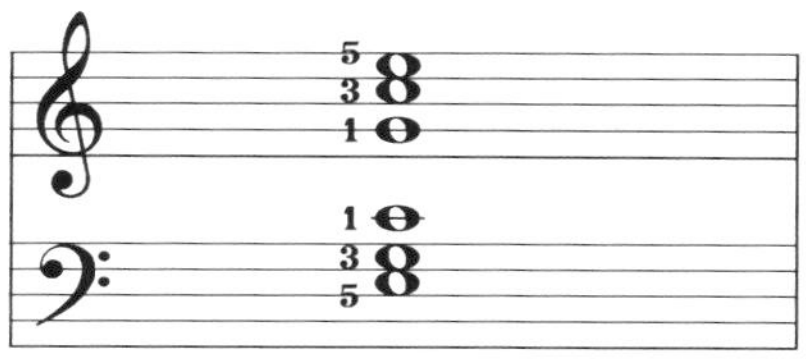

We can get different voicing and therefore different subtle colors by using different fingerings for the chord/inversion. Different fingerings will cause slightly different hand positions and angles. Every little tilt of the hand will influence the balance of the chord and produce a different sonority. An interesting and unique fingering that affects voicing is using the thumb on the middle note. This is not advisable when the middle note is a black key. The LH can do it in the root position and in the second inversion; the RH can do it in the root position and in the first inversion. For example, the chord C♯\E\A can be played in the RH with fingers 2\1\5 as shown in the following photo.

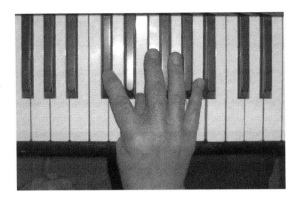

The chord E\A\C♯ can be played in the LH with fingers 5\1\2.

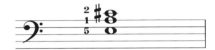

Often, circumstances require that we avoid either the thumb or the little finger in these chords or in any other three-note chord. This, like many other fingering situations, depends on where we are coming from into the chord and also where we are going to out of the chord, or if at the same time there are other notes to be held or played by the same hand. The most common use of this three-note chord alternative fingering is in the LH style of *Waltzes, Nocturnes, Ragtime, Marches*, or any music style where a bass note or a double octave bounces off against a chord or a number of chords. Harmonic intervals, such as octaves, thirds, etc., are usually referred to in piano playing as 'double intervals' when the two interval notes are played together in one hand, e.g., 'double octaves', 'double thirds', etc. In the music styles mentioned above, we avoid using finger 5 in the LH chords. Leaving finger 5 free to go down to the bass note/octave makes its traveling distance in both directions, from the bass note to the chord, and from the chord to the bass note, smaller than if we used it to play the chord. In the following picture the D minor triad chord in the root position is played by the LH with fingers 4\2\1 instead of 5\3\1, thus leaving the little finger free to have a head start with its travel toward the next bass note.

There are cases where the chord can be played with just fingers 3\2\1, thus letting the little finger get even closer to the next bass note.

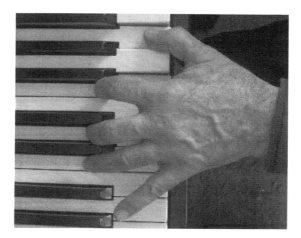

The above fingering might be desirable when the bass note and chord alternate quite rapidly, or when the bass note is quite far away, or when the chord's frame spans less than a perfect fifth, the latter of which can be seen in measure 6 of the Chopin *Waltz* example appearing in the next page.

Beware, although this tool is very useful and helpful, it should not be used "at any cost". Do not use it if the chord is better executed using the fifth finger, which could often be the case when it is a 7th chord. If any of the fingering stretches feel awkward or strenuous, don't use them.

Paderewski's *Menuet à l'Antique Op. 14, No. 1* sounds more like a *Waltz* in the *Brillante* section. Following is a LH fingering suggestion which avoids using the little finger in the chord. However, when we get to 7th chords, or any other chords that may feel strenuous, like in the last two measures of this example, we should reconsider our options, and choose fingering which will not hurt our hands. Measures 3-10 in the *Brillante* section:

With this fingering tool in mind, here is my suggestion for the LH fingering at the beginning of Chopin's *B minor Waltz Op. 69, No. 2*, measures 1-7.

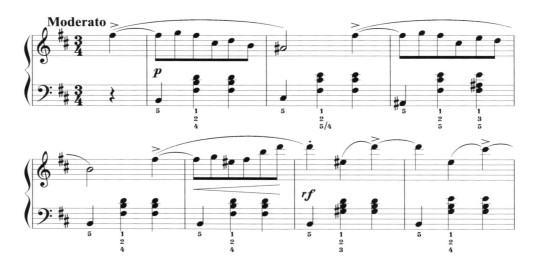

The next example conveys the same idea as it is used in the *F minor Nocturne Op. 55, No. 1* by Chopin, measures 1-2.

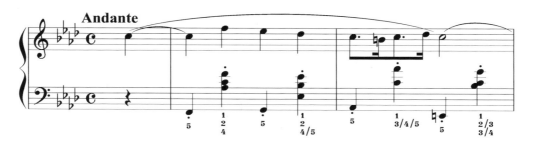

Now let us check this idea in the *Ragtime* style. Even though some of the bass notes are double octaves instead of just single notes, the idea of minimizing travel distance for the little finger is still valid. LH in measures 5-8 of *The Entertainer* by Scott Joplin:

The last example of this idea is Schubert, *Impromptu Op. 90, No. 4*, the LH in measures 39-42.

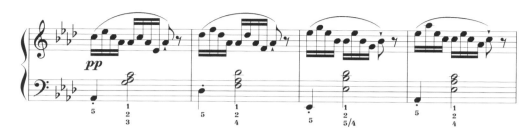

Related advice about technique: Play the bass notes with the wrist moving from the bottom up (the next top three photos, left to right), and play the chords with the wrist moving from top to bottom, thus creating wrist circles (bottom three photos, left to right).

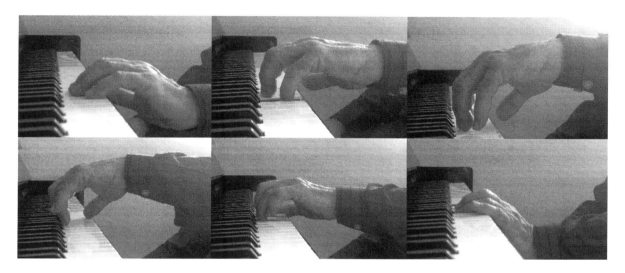

Four-note triad chords – root position

The right hand fingering is simple: 1\2\3\5.

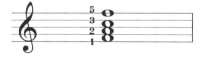

There is a standing debate though about the fingering of the left hand. The question is which finger should be used for the second note in the chord. Old books will mostly say the fourth finger.

Some more modern books and teachers will allow the third finger on some of these chords.

I personally prefer the third finger in most cases. Chords with all-white keys can be played with either the third finger or the fourth finger. The cases where I would use and recommend using the fourth finger are in the following minor chords: C, C♯, D♯, F, F♯, G, G♯, A♯, and B. Of course there is the notion that one fingering can fit one person's hand better than another's. That is true, although there is also another notion that in a way favors nurture over nature in this case, and says that hands grow and develop according to how they are used, so the way we learn and practice will eventually become the most comfortable way for us, or will eventually fit our hands best. In addition, there are various other factors which can affect the choice of fingering here, as in other cases: speed, chord sequences, dynamics, placement on the keyboard, and surroundings, which is what comes before the chord and after it, or how we get into the chord, and out of it. If we play D major followed by D minor in the LH, it would be quite fitting to use finger 3 on the F♯ in D major and finger 4 on the F♮ in D minor.

If we want this D minor chord in the LH played fortissimo, using finger 3 on the F might prove louder and safer than using finger 4. Playing the same D minor chord in the LH may feel different when played in various registers on the keyboard. In high octaves using finger 4 on F would feel less strenuous than finger 3 while in low octaves using finger 3 would feel better.

Four-note triad chords – inversions

Inversion fingerings in the LH do not present any problems. The first inversion fingering is 5\4\2\1 and the second inversion fingering is 5\3\2\1. Following is an example in G major for the LH in the first and the second inversions.

The first inversion in the RH does not present any problems either; the fingering is 1\2\4\5. Following is an example in C major for the RH first inversion.

The above debate arises again when we get to the second inversion of the RH. The question is which finger should be used on the third note of the second inversion (E in C major), finger 3, or finger 4.

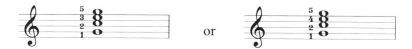

The second inversion of the RH mirrors in its shape the root position of the LH. The next example shows three sets of mirrored chord shapes. The RH mirrors the LH, and vice versa.

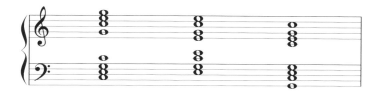

Here too I generally prefer the third finger in most cases. As a principle, I would mirror the keyboard picture of the chord and its fingering from the LH root position explanation which would sum it up as follows: Chords with all-white keys can be played with either finger 3 or finger 4. The cases where I would use and recommend using the fourth finger are the following major chords: C♯, D, E♭, E, F♯, A♭, A, B♭, and B.

The mirrored chord shapes in the above example are not perfectly mirrored if we check them on the keyboard. The LH keys C and E which are supposedly mirroring the RH keys E and G, do not have the same number of black keys between them. There are two black keys between C and E while there is only one black key between E and G.

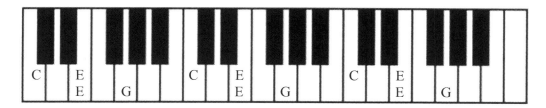

Furthermore, it may come as a surprise, but usually the white keys are not all the exact same width. The white keys within the groups of black keys (G, A, and D) are slightly wider than the two sets of neighboring white keys that do not have a black key between them (B, C, and E, F). These two tiny differences could also affect the fingering choices regarding the use of finger 3 or finger 4 in the relevant debated chord fingerings. Since the space between the keys C and E is a drop larger than the space between the keys E and G, one could choose to use finger 4 on E in the RH chord inversion G\C\E\G and finger 3 on E in the imperfectly mirrored LH chord C\E\G\C. An example of a perfect mirroring image on the keyboard would be the LH root position of C major, and the RH second inversion of A minor.

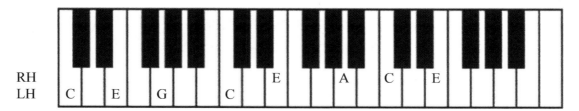

If I were to play the RH second inversion alternating between the two neighboring chords C major and D minor (all white keys), I would use finger 3 on E in the C major chord, and finger 4 on F in the D minor chord:

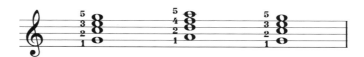

If I were to play the same D minor chord followed or preceded by a D major chord, I would use finger 3 on F♮ in the D minor chord, and finger 4 on F♯ in the D major chord:

Triad arpeggios and inversions

The above debates get a new angle with arpeggios. Unlike in chords where the hands are horizontally quite static, in arpeggios, the hands move horizontally on the keyboard. Due to this movement, choosing different fingering on the way down than on the way up can prove helpful. With every note we play in the arpeggio, we move the hand along to be right above the key which is being played and to get closer to and prepare the next note which is about to be played. This is the idea behind the following fingering suggestions. LH arpeggios in the root position for C major and other white-key arpeggios can be done with the fourth finger playing the second note on the way up and the third finger playing the same note on the way down, as shown in the following music example.

RH arpeggios in the second inversion for C major and other white-key arpeggios can be done with the third finger playing the third note of the inversion on the way up and the fourth finger playing the same note on the way down.

Arpeggios and their inversions give us a choice of more than one unique fingering. While not all of them may be perfectly fitting for every arpeggio and every inversion, theoretically we can use three different fingerings in each hand. When playing hands together, any of the RH fingerings can be matched with any of the LH fingerings. Furthermore, the following fingerings are all one needs to know in order to be able to finger any arpeggio and any inversion. One of these fingerings will be the perfect fit for the desired arpeggio/inversion:

   1.   We can start with the thumb in the RH and the little finger in the LH on each of the different arpeggio notes, thus playing in the RH 1-2-3(or 4)-5 (as the top end note) and in the LH 5-3(or 4)-2-1 (as the top end note).
   2.   We can start with finger 3 (or 4) on each of the different arpeggio notes in either hand, thus playing in the RH 3(or 4)-1-2 and in the LH 3(or 4)-2-1.
   3.   We can start with finger 2 on each of the different arpeggio notes in either hand, thus playing in the RH 2-3(or 4)-1 and in the LH 2-1-3(or 4).

These possibilities caused another little debate about the fingering of arpeggio inversions, especially the arpeggios with white keys. Some say we should start the inversions with the thumb in the RH and the little finger in the LH as we do when the tonic is a white key. Some others say we should always keep the original root position fingering, where the thumb in the RH and the little finger in the LH are always on the tonic note. In "my book" (pun intended), one needs to learn, practice, and master all three fingering possibilities mentioned above because in different situations any of these could prove to be the best choice.

The traditional fingering of the C major (and other similar keys) arpeggio in the root position, RH two octaves (and more), is 1-2-3-1-2-3-5 (we finish with the little finger instead of the thumb in order to avoid one extra and unnecessary crossing). The finger crossing tool is employed in the largest interval within the arpeggio, between G and C. This makes it quite awkward as can be seen in the next photo.

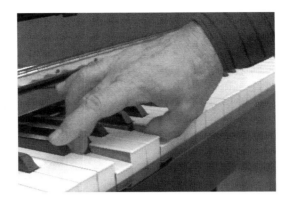

Not only is it awkward, but it is also impossible to play *legato* in a high speed. In a high speed we need to execute the arpeggio using the *non-legato* shifting technique, rather than plain *legato* crossing. I suggest that in various cases, as we may find fit, we can also use either of the other two fingerings for triad arpeggios:

　　1.　　4-1-2-4-1-2-4, which is also the fingering of C♯ major/minor arpeggio, as well as some other arpeggios starting on a black key. For convenience we actually start with finger 2 instead of finger 4.

　　2.　　2-4-1-2-4-1-2, which we use for some arpeggios in the second inversion:

　　The above alternative fingerings are better in the sense of not putting the finger crossing right at the largest interval of the arpeggio.

7th chords and inversions

　　We need to play four notes, and we have five fingers. The question we face is which four fingers we should use (rich people's problems...). We normally use fingers 1 and 2. Now the question narrows down to which fingers we should use on the remaining two notes: 4 and 5, 3 and 5, or 3 and 4. The answer depends on the particular type, or rather shape of the individual 7th chord or inversion. We should consider the stretch required between the fingers, and the length of the fingers, while trying to avoid an undesired twist of the hand. Following are some examples of mostly isolated 7th chords in the root position.

Some examples for the RH root position:
For C\E\G\B, I would use: 1\2\3\5.
For C\E\G\Bb, I would use: 1\2\3\5, or 1\2\3\4, or 1\2\4\5.
For C\Eb\G\Bb, I would use: 1\2\4\5.
For C\Eb\Gb\Bb, I would use: 1\2\3\5.
For C\Eb\G\B, I would use: 1\2\4\5.
For C\Eb\Gb\B, I would use: 1\2\3\5.
For C\Eb\Gb\A, I would use all 3 possibilities, depending on the surroundings and other factors: 1\2\3\5, or 1\2\3\4, or 1\2\4\5. There may even be cases where one will need to take this chord with fingers 2\3\4\5.

Some examples for the LH root position:
For C\E\G\B, I would use: 5\3\2\1.
For C\E\G\Bb, I would use: 5\3\2\1.
For C\Eb\G\Bb, I would use: 5\3\2\1, or 5\4\2\1.
For C\Eb\Gb\Bb, I would use: 5\3\2\1.
For C\Eb\G\B, I would use: 5\4\2\1.
For C\Eb\Gb\B, I would use: 5\3\2\1, or 5\4\2\1.
For C\Eb\Gb\A, I would use all 3 possibilities, depending on the surroundings and other factors: 5\3\2\1, or 5\4\2\1, or 4\3\2\1. There may even be cases where one will need to take this chord with fingers 5\4\3\2.

7th arpeggios and inversions

In one octave arpeggios and their inversions we use all five fingers successively. Here is one octave of C major Dominant 7th (G7) arpeggio and its three inversions.

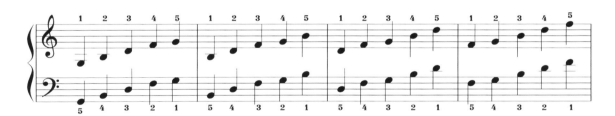

We can use this fingering also on black keys. Here is one octave of B major Dominant 7th (F♯7) arpeggio and its three inversions.

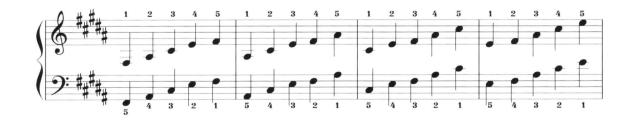

When we play more than one octave, here too, as with triad arpeggios, the inversions may follow the fingering of the root position, or start each inversion with the thumb in the RH, and the little finger in the LH, as we did above when we had only one octave. Theoretically, we have four possibilities of fingering. We can actually start each inversion in either hand with fingers 1, 2, 3, or 4, but not all of them are practical. When we play more than one octave arpeggios and inversions with black keys, we would be better off using the fingering principle which prevents the thumb from being played on a black key. In general, crossing with the thumb onto a black key, and in particular coming from a white key played with a non-thumb, and vice versa, is not recommended, unless we are in dire need of a *legato* articulation which cannot be achieved with any other fingering. Following is a photo of such an undesirable crossing.

Hand position for scales and arpeggios

The following recommendations are small deviations, not to be executed too rigidly and not to be exaggerated. Even if these small differences do not show physically, just thinking of them and feeling them alone will improve both the playing and the well-being of the hands:

1. Raise the hand slightly in a rotational movement at the side of the little finger. A rotational movement is the movement we do when we turn a door knob or a key in a door. The following photo on the left shows the LH somewhat collapsed at the little finger side before raising it. The photo on the right shows the hand raised at the little finger side:

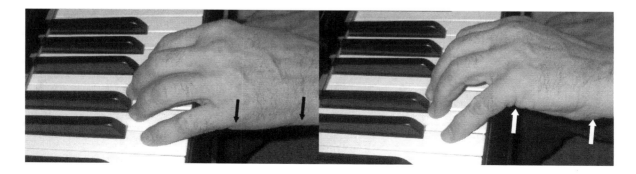

2.   Point the wrists slightly outwards (abduction, or radial flexion). The RH points the wrist to the right, and the LH points the wrist to the left. The following photo on the left shows the LH wrist somewhat pointing inwards (adduction, or ulnar flexion), something we should avoid. The photo on the right shows what we should do, the LH wrist pointing outwards (abduction):

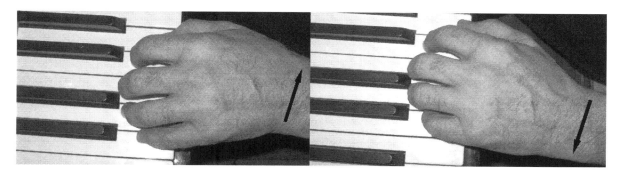

That said, I would generally advise that the hands stay aligned with the forearms (when viewed from above) as much as possible and wherever they travel on the keyboard.

3.   Keep the elbows slightly outwards, not touching the body. The RH elbow is kept slightly away from the body to the right, and the LH elbow is kept slightly away from the body to the left. At the same time also keep the elbows slightly forward of the body. The following photo on the left shows the LH elbow touching the side of the body, something we should normally avoid. The photo on the right shows the correct way of the elbow not touching the body:

As we play further at the extreme ends of the keyboard, our torso can move and tilt a little along with the arms in the same direction as our hands move on the keyboard. This works for each hand alone in either direction and for two hands together in the same direction. The torso does not need to move when both arms move on the keyboard in contrary motion.

Further Traditional, Advanced, and Innovative Fingering Tools

Blocking

Blocking groups of notes is generally a good way of learning music, practicing the piano, and memorizing. It is also very helpful in determining fingering. Blocking means playing together a group of notes that are written in succession, thus turning them into a chord. When the blocked notes are played as a chord, it is easier to allocate fingers to the notes than when the notes are played in succession as written. The first example is *Prelude No. 1 in C major* from *The Well Tempered Clavier, Book I*, by Bach. Let us look at the first 4 measures.

The 12 RH notes in each measure can be blocked into a single chord as follows:

The four LH notes in each measure can be blocked into a single chord as follows:

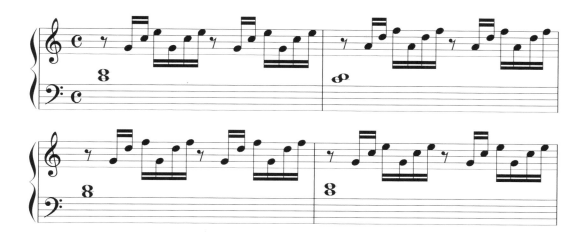

As a matter of fact, all the notes of both hands in each measure can be blocked into a single chord as follows:

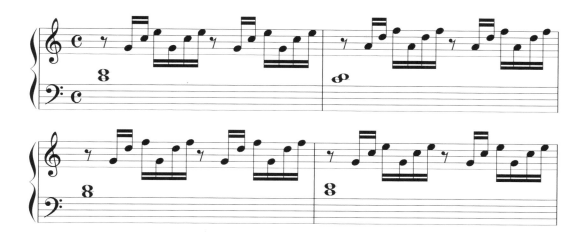

Now we have to finger only one chord per measure: three notes instead of twelve in the RH, and two notes instead of four in the LH. Fingering this single chord takes care of the fingering for the whole measure. But let us deal here with only the RH. We have a triad in the second inversion which, overall, spans the interval of a sixth. If we use the principle of expanding the five-finger position and skipping a key between the thumb and finger 2, we get the fingering of 1\3\5. The second measure has the same exact chord shape shifted one step higher, so we can again use the same fingering, just shifting the hand like a claw, moving one white key to the right. In the next chord only the bottom note, played with the thumb, changes, while the two top notes are the same as in the previous chord, and they keep the same fingering. What we get now is the same principle of expanding the five-finger position, this time skipping two keys between the thumb and the second finger. Measure 4 will naturally be fingered like measure 1.

A more advanced fingering of these four chords would derive from blocking all of them into a single double-blocked chord which has six notes.

We will finger this chord using the thumb on both bottom notes G and A: 1\2\3\4\5.

According to this double-blocked chord we can now finger the previous four blocked chords as follows:

The first, third, and fourth chords are fingered with the principle of expanding the five-finger position, skipping two keys between the thumb and the second finger. The second chord is fingered as before. Now we unblock the chords back to the original way in which the music is written and we keep each finger on its respective note. With this process we arrive at the following fingering for the RH in the first four measures of the *Prelude*.

Even though the above example for the RH has a finger written in for every note, the normal practice of editions is not to repeatedly write in fingering if the same passage or phrase or chord, etc., repeats. With this normal practice there would be no fingering indications in the fourth measure, as it is identical to the first one.

Of course, if there is a reason to use different fingering in the fourth measure it would be indicated. With this normal practice there would be no fingering indications in the second half of each measure either, as long as it is identical to the first half of the measure. Actually, even within the first half of the measure, the first three notes in the RH repeat themselves, so there is no need to write in fingering for the second group of three notes. In fact, all that needs to be indicated in the music for the RH is finger 2 on the note C. The rest is to be figured out according to the principles of the five-finger position and its expansions.

We saw two different fingerings in the RH for the first and fourth measures of the *Prelude* discussed above: 1-3-5 and 1-2-4. Both fingerings are valid and good. Personally, I prefer the first fingering of 1-3-5 as it automatically helps keep a better and healthier hand position.

The second blocking example is yet another Bach *Prelude* from *Book I, No. 5 in D major*. Let us examine the first measure in the RH.

All the RH notes in this entire measure can be blocked into a single chord.

This blocked chord has five notes; therefore it is fingered 1\2\3\4\5. Again, it is based on the principles of the five-finger position and its expansions. Between the thumb and the second finger there are two skipped keys, and between the fourth and fifth fingers there is one skipped key.

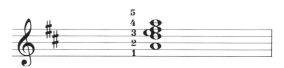

Unblocking the chord and keeping each finger on its respective note will give us the following:

The third example is Chopin, *Nocturne Op. 9, No. 2 in E♭ major*. Let us examine the LH in the first measure.

After the bass note in every group of three eighths, there are two chords that can be blocked into a single chord. Therefore, the LH fingering of the chords in this measure should be as follows:

The fourth example is the famous *G major Minuet, BWV 114* from the *Little Notebook for Anna Magdalena Bach*, composed by Christian Petzold (1677-1733).

All the LH notes in the first seven measures plus the first beat in the eighth measure can be blocked into a single chord which is within the five-finger position. Obviously, this chord will be fingered 5\4\3\2\1.

Therefore, the fingering for this LH section will be as follows:

The last example is the famous *Musette, BWV 126* from the *Little Notebook for Anna Magdalena Bach*. We are looking at the RH in the second part, the three measures that start eleven measures from the end. This example is a little less obvious at first glance because the groups of blocked notes do not correspond with the bar lines, nor with the rhythm or the seemingly obvious musical phrases. It is important to be able to spot, in any music, these types of groups of notes that can be blocked. In the next example each of the brackets marks a group of notes that can be blocked into a five-finger position chord. Not only does the following fingering for these two groups of notes give us the same fingers on the same notes in both octaves, but it will also help us phrase the music nicely with an upbeat (the eighth note D at the end of the second measure) by practically forcing us to get off the last note of the first bracket (A, played with the thumb), and shift the hand over to the first note of the next bracket (the upbeat D, played with finger 4).

Blocking segments of scales can improve the command of scale fingerings as well as speed. The following is a two-octave C major scale in contrary motion, blocked into four blocks according to the traditional C major scale fingering. This blocking idea can be used for other scales and their fingerings as well as for arpeggios and any inversions.

This brings to mind another thumb crossing exercise which derives from blocking the traditional C major scale fingering and can be adapted to other scales and arpeggios with their own fingerings. This exercise will help with remembering the scale fingering as well as with speed. Following is the exercise in two octaves of a contrary motion.

Let us look at the following zigzag arpeggio type, which skips a chord-note while moving in one direction, and goes back to the skipped chord-note while moving in the other direction. This passage creates two melodic lines going in the same direction: the bottom line consisting of the notes C, E, G, etc., and the top line consisting of the notes G, C, E, etc.

Blocking this zigzag arpeggio type into chords will help finger the passage. There are basically three ways of doing it:

1.   Blocking according to inversions, which means that in triad arpeggios (arpeggios with three different notes) we block every four notes, thus getting three different blocked chords in the following order: root position, second inversion, and first inversion. As a result the same fingering is not repeated in every octave but in every other octave, not at all a disadvantage according to my views.

2.   Forming an expanded block which includes six notes with the same four fingers. This means that the thumb will be used for two successive notes in the bottom melodic line, and the top melodic-line note in between these two successive bottom-line notes will be played with finger 2. The little finger can also be used for two successive top-line notes but it is a little less practical. When creating fingering according to this idea, it is wiser to have the stretch between the thumb and finger 2 where the interval is a fifth rather than where the interval is a sixth. Therefore, in the following example the thumb on C will be followed by finger 2 on G, and then the thumb on E will be followed by finger 4 on the C one octave higher. It is not

physically possible for the above to be played together as a chord, but it's still considered a block because the other three fingers can remain stationary while the thumb moves between its two notes. This fingering idea enables the same fingering in every octave, not necessarily a great advantage in my opinion, but definitely a good fingering tool to have.

Expanded block:
Interval of a fifth:

3. The following divides the expanded six-note block into two blocks: one made up of four notes and the other made up of two notes (one note, G in this case, appears in both blocks). Also this fingering repeats itself in every octave.

4-note block:
2-note block:

The above fingering possibilities numbers 2 and 3, where the fingering is consistent in every octave, repeat themselves every six notes and might be more suitable for a passage appearing in a triple meter as shown in the next example.

The above three ways of blocking and fingering this type of a zigzag arpeggio are useful in many cases. The following example is one such RH case from Beethoven's *Concerto No. 5 in E♭ major, Op. 73*. The passage is the beginning of the third *Solo* section in the first movement, and the fingering choice appearing in this example is the first out of the three mentioned above. All three fingering possibilities shown above are valid and good here. I personally prefer the first possibility as it requires the least number of times using and moving the thumb as well as consistently moving it every four notes and not sooner. In this particular passage we have two extra notes added towards the end of it, and interrupting the sequence. Having the extra notes, C at the end of the third beat, and F at the beginning of the fourth beat in the second measure of the example, enables us to include them in either of the blocked chords, and of course finger them accordingly. These two notes can belong to the blocked chord that follows them (fingering above the notes), or to the one that precedes them (fingering under the notes).

Patterns and sequences

Noticing patterns and sequences is known to be good for sight reading and memorization. Looking for, and finding patterns and sequences, can also be very helpful with fingering. Patterns and sequences are not always obvious. They can be hidden when they do not necessarily correspond with the rhythmic structure, the beat, the bar line, or the musical phrase. Some patterns can be pretty long, and therefore also hard to spot in a sequence. Small patterns can appear within a bigger pattern, and small sequences can appear within a bigger sequence. Nonidentical and incomplete patterns can also form a sequence – an imperfect one. A pattern doesn't necessarily have to be what it seems at first glance. We can shift the beginning of a pattern from the first note to any other note in the group of notes. Examples of obvious patterns and sequences are the famous Hanon finger exercises. Let us examine *Exercise No. 1*.

3 patterns:
Sequence:

Each pattern is made of eight notes. The first pattern consists of the notes C-E-F-G-A-G-F-E. It follows the diatonic intervals of an ascending skip and three steps, then three descending steps. While only five of the eight notes in the pattern are different notes (C, E, F, G, A), all eight notes in the pattern span the interval of a sixth (C to A). Therefore, they can be played with one expanded five-finger position: In the RH fingers 1-2-3-4-5-4-3-2, the skipped key is between fingers 1 and 2; in the LH fingers 5-4-3-2-1-2-3-4, the skipped key is between fingers 5 and 4. The second and third patterns have the same horizontal image of the skip and steps as the first pattern and each of them starts one step higher than the previous one, thus forming a sequence. Since the second and third patterns in the sequence have the same horizontal image, we can apply the same fingering that we used on the first pattern. This is shown in the following example.

Here is an example of hidden patterns and a sequence.

There are three similar patterns in this sequence, each starting one step higher than the previous one. Each of the patterns consists of four notes regardless of their placement in the measure or over the bar line and regardless of their rhythmic value. These patterns have the same horizontal image as far as the diatonic intervals are concerned. It is easier to see them if we ignore the rhythm and the bar lines. The first pattern consists of the notes C-E-A-G, the second pattern is D-F-B-A, and the third is E-G-C-B. Now it will be easy to finger this whole passage. As in the previous example, the first pattern spans a sixth, and is within the expanded five-finger position. Therefore, it will be fingered 1-2-5-4 in the RH and 5-3-1-2 in the LH. The remaining two patterns in the sequence will be fingered the same way.

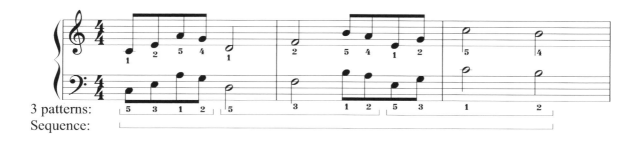

In *Solfeggietto* by Carl Philipp Emanuel Bach, measures 13 and 14 are a pattern that is repeated in measures 15 and 16. Each of these patterns is two-measures long, and together they form a four-measure long sequence – measure 13 to measure 16:

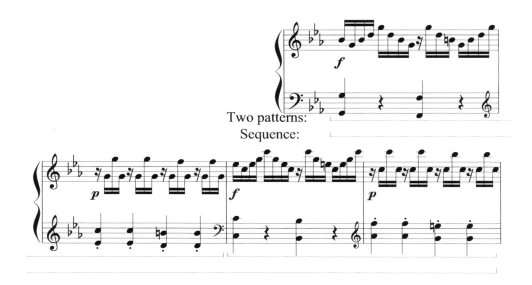

Measure 6 of Rachmaninov, *Prelude Op. 3, No. 2 in C# minor*, has the patterns as chords in groups of two eighth notes, and four of these groups make a sequence.

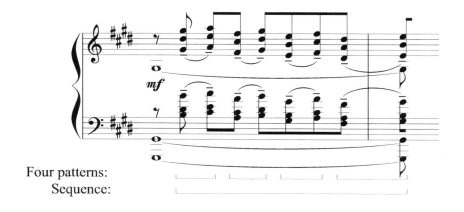

Continuing to measure 7, we see the same sequence again, but this time it starts a third lower than the previous one. This turns what we just referred to as a sequence into a big pattern, and the bigger sequence encompasses both measures 6 and 7.

Tchaikovsky's *February, No. 2* from *The Seasons Op. 37a*, also has small patterns within bigger ones and small sequences within bigger ones. Measure 9 is a pattern that is repeated in measure 10, thus forming a sequence. However, when we continue along, we realize that measures 9-12 are also a pattern, one that is four-measure long. This pattern is repeated in the following four measures, thus creating a large sequence of all eight measures, 9-16.

It is quite hard to tell where the big patterns are, and therefore where the big sequence is in measures 46-51 of Chopin's *E major Étude Op. 10, No. 3*. Yes, the first four sixteenth notes make a pattern that is repeated in the next four sixteenths, thus creating a sequence. And yes, the following four sixteenth notes make a little different pattern, which is repeated in the next four sixteenths, thus creating a new sequence, somewhat different than the first one. But, seeing that alone would be seeing only the small picture. The big picture tells us that the two sequences we just noticed in measures 46-47 are just the first big pattern out of three that make this a long sequence of six measures, 46-51. Seeing the big picture here may not only affect the fingering choice but also help to learn the passage, understand it musically, and memorize it. Of course one can play the entire passage with one fingering pattern of 2\5-1\3-1\3-2\5 in the RH and 5\2-3\1-3\1-5\2 in the LH, but there is also another fingering which will help distinguish between the first and the second small sequences of eight sixteenth notes, as shown in the following example:

Small patterns:
Small sequences:
3 big patterns:
Big sequence:

We can see nonidentical patterns forming an imperfect sequence in the first three measures of the *Preludio* from *Bachianas Brasileiras No. 4* by Villa-Lobos. The difference in the RH is very small; the third eighth note of the second measure is not a skip up from the previous note but a step up.

Small difference:
Nonidentical patterns:
Sequence:

Patterns may fit into a single hand position or be spread over more than a single hand position. They can be divided between the two hands in one horizontal continuation as well as appear vertically together. Often the same fingering may fit all the patterns through the entire sequence, as we see in the next two examples. Bach, *Italian Concerto, BWV 971*, first eight measures:

Two identical patterns:
Sequence:

Chopin, *second Sonata, Op. 35*, fourth movement, first two measures:

Two identical patterns:
Sequence:

But, we have to recognize the patterns and the sequence even if they are not obvious at first glance. Measure 66 in Debussy's *Clair de Lune* from *Suite Bergamasque* is not written in a way that catches the eye as two patterns that make a sequence, but they are. Recognizing that will help us finger this passage: fingers 5-2-1 in the LH for the first three sixteenths, and fingers 1-2-5 in the RH for the second three sixteenths. That is, in each group of six sixteenths as shown next.

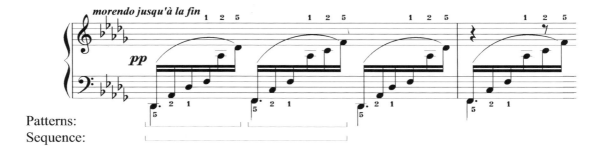

Patterns:
Sequence:

This type of fingering consistency, where a fingering can be repeated in identical patterns or in other similar passages, is of course a very useful tool, but it is not necessarily always an advantage. Many cases may actually benefit from different fingerings for similar passages. Different fingerings for similar passages may be necessary due to keyboard topography, actual text, and what happens immediately before and after the passage. These fingering inconsistencies can also be helpful with variety of sound, voicing, articulation, timing, agility, phrasing, memory, etc.

In Albéniz, *Asturias – Leyenda* from *Suite española*, measures 38-41 of the middle section marked *Più lento*, we can use the same fingering for the two RH patterns. Even though this is theoretically possible, I would not recommend doing so in the LH due to the appearance of black keys in different spots of the two otherwise very-similar patterns. Here is my recommended fingering for both hands in this sequence.

Patterns:
Sequence:

In Handel's *Passacaglia* from *Suite No. 7*, measures 9-12, we can use the same fingering for the four LH patterns, but the keyboard topography dictates otherwise for the RH fingering as shown in the next example.

4 patterns:
Sequence:

The following example is a passage from *Prelude No. 1* by Gershwin, measure 20. Using fingers 2 and 3 alternately for the middle note in the RH groups of three notes improves the execution of this passage in many respects. The same goes for the similar passage in measure 29. Alternating the middle notes with fingers 2 and 3 gives a better grasp of the passage as these fingers act here like a pivoting anchor. This fingering does not follow the immediate consistency in every three-note group of the little patterns, but it does follow a consistency of a larger group of six notes in a larger pattern. Actually the note patterns are in groups of three notes while the fingering patterns are in groups of six notes.

This notion of looking at bigger patterns and larger groups of notes goes along with the important musical notion of creating longer phrases rather than the immediate obvious small ones.

Note patterns:
Fingering patterns:
Sequence:

Chopin's *Étude Op. 10, No. 1* has quite obvious RH four-note patterns that determine the fingering groups of 1-2-4-5 and 1-2-3-5. The first four sixteenth notes form the first pattern, and it can be blocked by a "medium-large" hand span. The frame interval of this block is a major tenth while some of the patterns in the piece span an even larger interval. The use of some black keys in the various chord combinations and the intervals between the notes within the patterns can be strenuous for the small hand. Of course we do not need to actually play these patterns as blocked chords, and the small hand can also do a great job on this *Étude* using the technical concept that the hand moves along to constantly be over the playing finger. Following are the first two measures with the standard fingering.

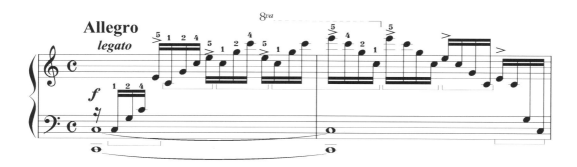

Regardless of hand size and stretching ability, I suggest exploring other four-note patterns within these passages, and therefore other fingering possibilities which can come in very handy in some of the passages of this *Étude*. If we see the four-note pattern as starting on the second sixteenth note, which is G in the first passage, we can use the fingering group 1-2-4-2. This means that we will begin with finger 2 on C and cross to the thumb on G. Theoretically, this fingering idea, of starting the four-note pattern on the second sixteenth note of the measure and putting the thumb on it, can fit the entire *Étude*. This does not mean it is recommended for the entire *Étude*, but it can be very useful for some of the passages in this *Étude*.

Even though we can, choosing to use this new fingering on any ascending passage does not mean we need to descend the same way. We may choose to use the new fingering on the way up and return with the traditional fingering. There are two passages in this *Étude* where we cannot use the alternative fingering shown above because the second note of the passage is a black key and playing it with the thumb will not work well in this case. These passages can benefit from moving the four-note pattern even further, to the third sixteenth note of the passage, on which we will put the thumb. These two passages are measure 31,

and measure 65.

Often appearing in scores is the sequence of a zigzag scale in broken thirds that moves a skip in one direction and a step in the other direction as shown in the next example.

In order to be able to finger it, one has to determine a number of things first. One has to decide whether the fingering group should be a two-note pattern, a four-note pattern, a six-note pattern, or even an eight-note pattern. One also has to decide on which note of the passage the pattern begins. Like in everything else, here too, one has to consider the rhythm, the meter, the phrasing, the desired articulation, and the keyboard topography. A two-note pattern of fingering would serve us best when the notes are slurred in pairs. Slurred pairs that make up the two-note patterns can appear as intervals of thirds or as intervals of seconds. The next example is from the *Allegro* (the first movement) of Mozart, *Sonata in G major K. 283*, measures 16 through 18. Mozart did not indicate a change of dynamics since the last *forte* he marked, so one may choose to play these ascending passages pretty vigorously, within Mozart style of course. If not played vigorously, perhaps they can be played in the manner of *basso buffo*. Either way, slurring the notes in pairs of thirds would be quite fitting here, and thus we have the following fingering. Actually, even if one wants to play these passages softly, the following two-note phrases are still a nice articulation choice. Two fingering possibilities are shown, and either of them can serve the same purpose.

Two-note patterns:

Slurring this type of zigzag scale sequence in pairs of seconds is the way Mozart phrased the third measure RH in the *Allegretto grazioso* (the third movement) of his *Sonata in B♭ major, K. 333*. Therefore, the suggested fingering for this ascending passage is as follows:

Two-note patterns: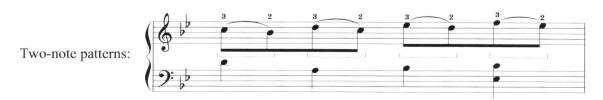

In long passages of more than one octave in one direction, a two-note pattern of fingering will be consistent and will keep the same fingering for every octave. This two-note pattern of fingering can also serve us without slurring the notes in pairs. Beethoven used it four times in the *Adagio grazioso* (the second movement) of his *Sonata Op. 31, No. 1*. With this fingering he wanted to achieve a very light and even touch for these long ascending passages. Following is measure 10 of the *Adagio*.

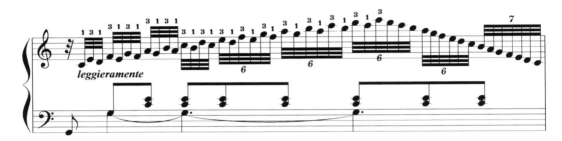

All the following fingering groups dealing with this type of zigzag scales in broken thirds derive from the fingerings of scales in double thirds as will be discussed later on. A four-note pattern of fingering 1-3-2-4, and in the opposite direction 4-2-3-1, is the most commonly used for this type of zigzag scale. It enables speed and brilliance. Some editions recommend this fingering also for the above passage. In long passages of more than one octave in one direction this fingering does not repeat itself on the same notes in the second octave; however, it does repeat in the third octave. Following is another Beethoven example; this time it is the last RH *Cadenza* in the *Allegro* (the third movement) of *Concerto No. 3*, right before the *Presto Coda* in the time signature of 6/8 that ends the movement and the whole *Concerto*. Here there is a sweeping consensus that there is no better fingering than the four-note pattern 1-3-2-4 for this long ascending virtuosic passage.

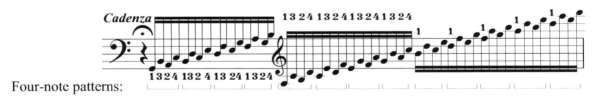

Four-note patterns:

A six-note pattern 1-3-2-4-3-5, and in the opposite direction 5-3-4-2-3-1, can be useful when we want to have the fingering correspond with a triple meter for the pairs of notes or when we want to avoid the thumb playing on a black key. In long passages of more than one octave in one direction this fingering will repeat itself on the same notes only in the fourth octave. The *Allegro* (the first movement) of Mozart's *D major Sonata K. 576* is written in a 6/8 meter. Measure 7 has this ascending zigzag scale which would fit nicely with the six-note pattern 1-3-2-4-3-5. Add to it the bottom half of a wrist circle movement, which is counter-clockwise for the RH, and you will get a beautifully shaped passage.

Six-note pattern:

This six-note pattern can help us avoid the thumb on black keys in the RH ascending passage of the following example: Mozart, *Sonata in E♭ major K. 282*, the *Adagio* (the first movement), measure 15 (end of the exposition). Another version of the six-note pattern is the fingering group 1-2-1-3-2-4, and in the opposite direction 4-2-3-1-2-1. This extra version of fingering the six-note pattern will be given as another option in the next example. One more important notion, as we can see in the next example, is that a pattern group of fingering does not necessarily have to start at the beginning of the given passage. It is our job to determine where we want our fingering patterns to begin.

Six-note patterns:

An eight-note pattern is quite rare, but it is possible and useful when fitting. It can help us avoid the use of the thumb on a black key. For fingering an eight-note pattern we would combine the two versions of a six-note pattern, thus getting the fingering groups of 1-2-1-3-2-4-3-5, and in the opposite direction 5-3-4-2-3-1-2-1. In long passages of more than one octave in one direction this fingering will repeat itself on the same notes only in the fifth octave. This eight-note pattern can serve the RH passage in measures 3 and 4 of the *Allegro* (the third movement) of the same *Sonata* as above, Mozart's *K. 282*.

Eight-note pattern:

If we want fingering consistency in every octave of a long passage in the same direction, we can combine different pattern groups of fingering. Two four-note patterns and one six-note pattern in any order of succession will give us this consistency. One six-note pattern and one eight-note pattern in any order of succession will also give us this consistency. This fingering consistency may not be the preferred fingering everywhere, and it cannot correspond with any even metrical division of the note-groups, but it can certainly have its merits as shown in the next example. Liszt, *Mephisto Waltz*, the descending RH passage at the end of the long measure *Cadenza*, 99 measures from the end of the piece:

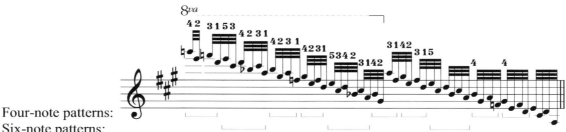

Four-note patterns:
Six-note patterns:

Some people may choose to play the above passage with two hands in *Toccata style*, where the top notes are played with the RH, and the bottom notes are played with the LH, as shown in the next example.

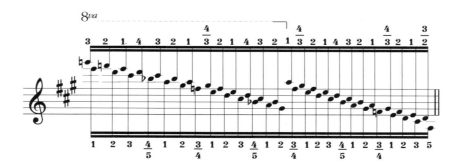

Whether we should use the thumb on a black key or not is a choice we have to make while understanding that avoiding the thumb on a black key is not necessarily always the best choice.

The last passage to be discussed under this topic is Beethoven, *Sonata in E major Op. 109*, first movement, measures 6 and 7 of the second *Adagio espressivo*. The entire passage can be played with the six-note pattern of fingering 5-3-4-2-3-1 in the right hand, and 1-3-2-4-3-5 in the left hand. This fingering would correspond with the triple meter. The entire passage can also be played in both hands with a combination of two fingering groups: a six-note pattern and an eight-note pattern in either order of succession, which gives us two extra consistent fingerings in every octave. All three fingering possibilities are presented in the next example, one fingering set is above the notes and the other two sets are below the notes. The two fingering sets below the notes can be mixed and matched between the hands.

RH six-note patterns:

RH combined patterns:

LH six-note patterns:

LH combined patterns:

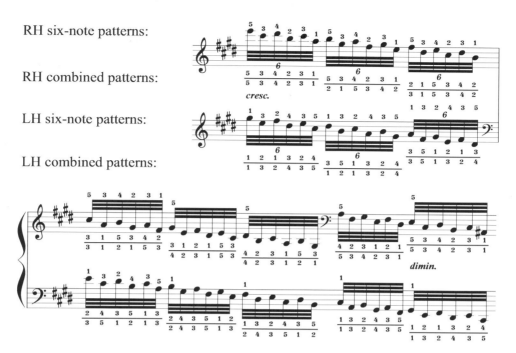

If you don't care for the thumb and the little finger playing on black keys in this passage and you are not happy using your weak fingers, perhaps the following fingering will be your preferred solution. There are various other fingering combinations and possibilities for this passage, but let us examine what the following gives us. It is consistent in every octave, except for the very last RH note in the passage which changes from A to A♯. It employs a fingering group that consists of a four-note pattern, twice per octave, and a fingering group that consists of a two-note pattern, three times per octave. It does not have the thumb playing on black keys and it does not use the little finger at all. Even though it does not correspond with the triple meter, it does not upset it either.

RH four-note patterns:
RH two-note pattern:

LH four-note patterns:
LH two-note patterns:

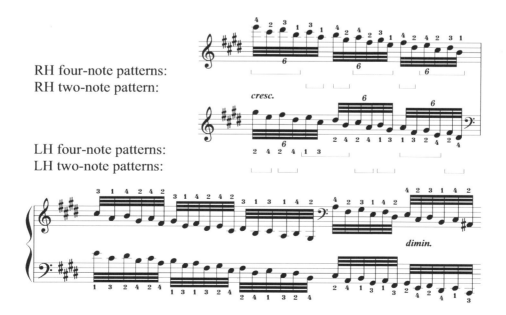

Figuring out fingering backwards

Often we have to figure out fingering backwards. The next little RH phrase demonstrates it.

If we just try C major scale fingering, we will get stuck when we get to the first A with finger 3. How about F major scale fingering? We also get stuck on the first A with finger 2. We must decide what finger to put on this first A before we finger the previous notes. Since from this A there is a jump of an octave up to another A, we will put the thumb on this first A, the lower one, and the little finger on the second A, the higher one.

Now that we know the thumb must be on the first A, we can work the rest of the fingering backwards. Here we have various possibilities, one of them is: finger 3 on G, finger 2 on F, finger 1 on E, finger 3 on D, finger 2 on C. This fingering and two more possibilities are shown in the following example, though there are other possibilities too.

Another example of working the fingering backwards is the next little RH phrase. We don't know what finger to put on the starting note C unless we figure out first what finger we need on the third note E. Since this E jumps an octave down to another E, we will put the little finger on it. Now we can work the other fingering back from the little finger E and put finger 4 on D and finger 3 on C.

One more example is the following C major scale in the RH. It starts on the middle C and ascends up to D, an interval of a ninth above the middle C. If we play the C major fingering, we would need to cross the thumb twice. If we put the little finger on the last note D and work the fingering back, we can come up with the following fingering which requires only one crossing of the thumb.

Sliding

After playing on a black key we do not need to lift our finger off it and we can play the adjacent white key (a half step / semitone) on either side by sliding our finger from the black key to the neighboring white key. This will create *legato* playing with just one finger. It is as if we are gaining an extra finger – a sixth finger in the same hand – and we can maintain the same hand position without any thumb crossing. We can do this slide with any finger on any black key. Theoretically, we can achieve *legato* playing of ten notes: five black keys and five of their adjacent white keys in either direction, playing each pair with just one finger as if we have ten fingers in one hand. Notice that no change of hand position is necessary nor any thumb crossing. This fingering technique will also help if we wish to keep holding down some of these white keys as we do in finger pedaling. The following examples can also be used as sliding exercises.

RH sliding example/exercise:

LH sliding example/exercise:

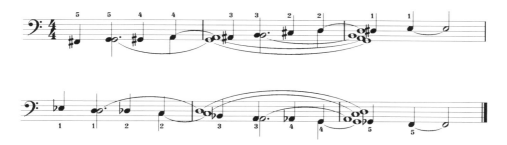

Finger sliding is very useful in any music, whether in Bach's *Fugues*, where we always seem to need extra fingers, or in romantic and modern music. In the third measure of Chopin's *Étude Op. 10, No. 4* there is a repeated RH pattern which seems to go well all four times with the fingering pattern of 1-2-5-3. However, considering the *Presto* tempo, moving from the last RH note of the measure (which is E played with finger 3) to the C♯ double octave at the beginning of the next measure is not going to be very smooth. If we take finger 2 on this E (the last RH note of the measure) we will have a better transition to the following C♯ double octave, and at the same time, by using the sliding technique from a black key to a white key, we won't lose the *legato* of the inner voice from the previous D♯ to this E.

Changing fingers on a held note (substituting)

Finger substitution technique is a very useful tool which enables us to play *legato* on more keys than a single hand position can offer us and without any thumb crossing. It is again as if our hand is gaining extra fingers. Substituting a finger on a held note can be done in either direction, from a lower number finger to a higher one and vice versa. It can be done with an adjacent finger as well as by skipping a finger or more. Substituting a finger on a held note can also be done with a finger of the other hand. Finger substitution is a very common tool in organ playing, as the organ does not have a sustain pedal, and all *legato* has to be accomplished just by the fingers playing on the keys alone. Even though we can use the sustain pedal to help us play *legato*, real *legato* playing should first be achieved, just like in organ playing, with no use of the sustain pedal. Some musicians play Bach, Haydn, and Mozart with no pedal at all or with very little pedal. The ability to play a pure finger *legato* is of great importance in piano playing. For example, if we need to play a right hand *legato* of the same note in three consecutively ascending octaves, we will use fingers 1 and 5, then substitute finger 5 with finger 1, and then again play with finger 5. The following example uses the note C in three consecutively ascending octaves. The finger substitution happens on the second C of the three. Fingering notation often uses a dash between two finger numbers to indicate substitution. Some notations use a little slur over the two relevant finger numbers.

Another examples is *Ah! vous dirai-je, Maman* – also known as *Twinkle, Twinkle, Little Star*. If we play it in C major we get with finger 4 to the half note G in the second measure where the word "star" falls. If we substitute finger 4 with finger 5 on this G, we can continue the descent to C, playing *legato* without using finger-crossing or condensing the hand, nor any further use of other fingering tools.

Here is an example of finger substitution in the RH from the very first chord of Beethoven, *D minor Sonata Op. 31, No. 2*, the *Tempest*. In this opening *Largo*, the first half note chord written in the bass clef is played by the RH.

Below are useful exercises for substituting fingers. Play each hand alone and each fingering alone. The fingerings for the RH are written above the notes, and the fingerings for the LH are written underneath the notes.

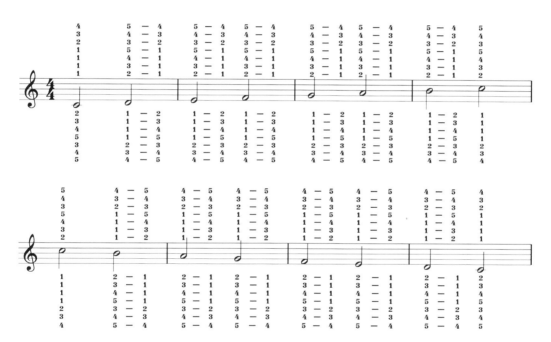

The above exercises are written in C major, thus using only the white keys. Similar exercises can also be made in different keys, on black keys alone, and in chromatic scales.

In many cases we may also find the need to substitute with a finger in the other hand. We play a note with a finger in one hand and then substitute it with a finger in the other hand. This technique can come in very handy in playing *Fugues* by Bach where the middle voices are played alternately by either hand. Of course it can also be used with any music from other composers and periods, whether polyphonic or not. In Chopin's *Scherzo No. 2, Op. 31* we may find the need to substitute with the other hand. In the middle section, 29 measures after the double bar line and the change of key signature to three sharps, the thumb of the LH can substitute the thumb of the RH on the tied note F♯. But, in order to be able to do it, we need to prepare with a couple of other previous substitutions in the LH. Here are measures 25-29 of the middle section.

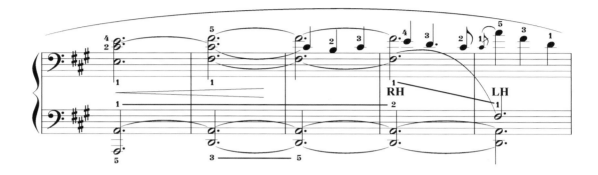

Actually, following the way it is written in the music we will not be able to execute it correctly. We need to substitute with the thumb of the LH on the F♯ sooner than it says in this score. Only then will we get the tied F♯ properly held. The following example puts this particular substitution on the third beat of measure 28, but it can be put earlier, as early as the first beat in measure 27. This means that the preparatory substitutions in the LH will also have to be done earlier.

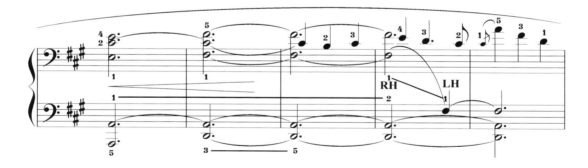

This tool is very useful in Chopin's *Fantasie Op. 49* and can be used quite a few times in similar places of the piece. Measures 43-44 will serve as a small example.

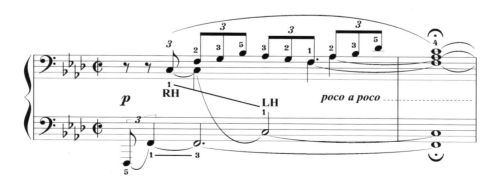

One finger on two or more keys

One finger on two keys is often done with the thumb on two adjacent white keys. We play the thumb "in the crack" between the two white keys, thus pressing both keys simultaneously.

In various cases it would be more comfortable to play two neighboring keys together with the thumb alone rather than with fingers 1 and 2. The reason is that in certain note-combinations and certain chords, playing fingers 1 and 2 on two neighboring keys can cause an unpleasant stretch. I'll use the chord C\D\F♯\B in the RH as an example. Instead of fingering it 1\2\3\5, which can cause an unpleasant stretch, we can use the thumb on both C and D together, finger 2 on F♯, and finger 5 on B.

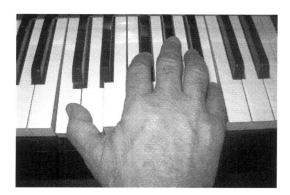

The written music marking of one finger playing two notes will usually be the finger number inside or outside a little bracket showing the two notes or without a bracket. It will appear either horizontally on either side of the notes or vertically. Various marking possibilities are shown in the next example.

Debussy uses this fingering tool a lot in the famous *Prelude No. 10* of the *first Book, La Cathédrale engloutie* (*The Sunken Cathedral*). The next example is measures 42-45. In the second chord the RH plays C and D doubled up in two octaves. There is practically no other way to finger this chord than with the thumb playing both bottom notes C and D together.

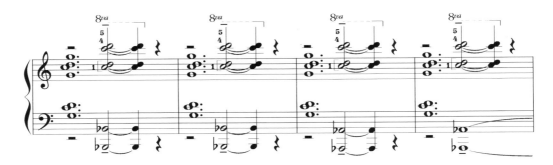

This tool can also be useful when we play the LH style of *Ragtime, March, Waltz, Nocturne,* or any bass note bouncing off against a chord or two. There are cases where we would want to finger a chord with the thumb playing simultaneously on the two top notes of the chord when they are adjacent and executable in this manner. Let us look at the LH, second beat in the third measure of Chopin, *Nocturne Op. 9, No. 2 in E♭ major*. We have a bass note followed by two chords that continue to the next bass note. The fingering which will allow the least amount of hand travel, thus making it more secure to execute, would be as follows: the little finger on the bass notes, fingers 4\1 on the G\F harmonic interval, and fingers 2\1 on the D\F\G chord, that is, finger 2 on D and the thumb on both F and G.

We can also use this fingering tool for the left hand in measure 42 of Mozart's *Rondo Alla Turca* (*Turkish March*) from the *A major Sonata K. 331*. The following example shows measures 41-44.

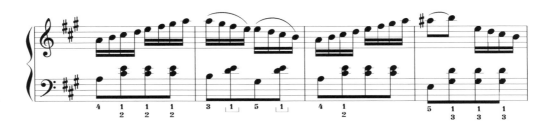

Another example is my own *Breezy Rider Rag*, measures 6 and 7 in the LH. I repeatedly use this type of LH accompaniment in this piece. The fingering that will enable the shortest traveling distance for the hand would be fingers 3 and 5 alternating on the bass notes B and G, and the thumb on both of the two top notes F and G together. This fingering is free of strenuous stretches, thus making the execution of the accompaniment more secure and healthy.

The thumb can play simultaneously on two adjacent black keys too. Here we need to somewhat extend the thumb beyond its normal position so we can press both black keys simultaneously.

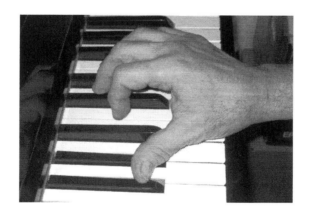

The same Debussy *Prelude* as above, *La Cathédrale engloutie,* employs this tool as well. We find an example of both hands in the first chord of measure 17 that repeats itself also in measure 18. The two top notes of the chord in the LH are the black keys F♯\G♯ which are played with the LH thumb. The two bottom notes of the chord in the RH are the black keys F♯\G♯ which are played with the RH thumb.

The thumb can also play simultaneously on two black keys which are separated by two white keys – a step and a half apart.

This is quite rare, but interestingly, it can be helpful in playing the big chord in measure 12 of *Prelude Op. 28, No. 7* by Chopin. That is, of course, if one can reach this particular frame interval of a minor tenth in the first place.

It is quite rare to use any other finger on two adjacent keys; yet there are some cases in the literature where one finger, other than the thumb, is used on two adjacent white keys. In order to execute it, we play like we do with the thumb on two adjacent white keys. We play "in the crack" between the two white keys, thus pressing both keys simultaneously.

In the same *Prelude, La Cathédrale engloutie*, Debussy makes use of this tool. We find it in measure 26 in the first chord of the RH, and it also repeats at the beginning of measure 27. The chord starts on the middle C, and is composed of the bottom to top notes C\D\F\G\A\D. It may be possible to finger this chord with the thumb on both C and D, finger 2 on F, finger 3 on G, finger 4 on A, and finger 5 on D. But, for most people this would, at best, be a very unpleasant stretch. The tool of using finger 2 on two keys together enables us to finger this chord with the thumb on both C and D, finger 2 on both F and G, finger 3 on A, and finger 5 on D. This fingering is much more comfortable for the hand, and, more importantly, it is much healthier for the hand.

The next example utilizes this tool in the most unusual and unique way. It is the famous passage which appears four times towards the end of the *Allegro, ma non troppo* (the third movement) of Prokofiev's *Concerto No. 3*. Each time is a series of repeated ascending and descending quasi scale/arpeggio passages with alternating hands. The main component of this passage is pairs of adjacent notes played together which have to be played with one finger per pair because, otherwise, we don't have enough fingers in our hands to cover the whole passage as written. The LH fingers 4, 2, and 1 play each on a different pair of keys, while the RH fingers 1, 2, 3, and 4 also play each on a different pair of keys. Two out of the four times the passages start on the note C, and the other two times they start on the note G. They are all only white keys, and therefore it is possible to use this fingering tool. The next example shows the beginning of the passage that starts on the note C.

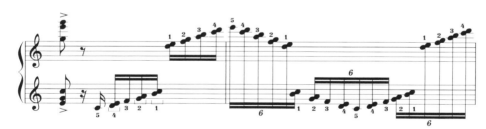

These above passages are quite tricky and may be strenuous for the small-span hand. Some pianists solve this problem by rewriting the passage as follows, or in a similar way.

Since these passages are on white keys only and sound like ascending and descending *glissandos*, some pianists choose to actually execute them as such. The most effective way of executing a glissando here would be by using the RH, both for ascending and descending, while the LH plays the bottom note C and the top note E.

A non-thumb finger on two adjacent black keys is not used in the standard repertoire. It is also quite rare to use one finger on three adjacent keys, but the thumb can do that. In order to simultaneously press on all three keys we need to extend the thumb beyond its normal position. Theoretically, all we need to do is cover the two cracks between the three keys, but if we want more power, we need to cover the surface of all three keys more evenly. The following photo shows the thumb playing on three white keys.

We find the thumb playing simultaneously on three neighboring white keys in a number of cases in the *Allegro molto* (the third movement) of the Bartók *Sonata* from 1926. Bartók uses this fingering tool in each of the hands. The next example shows the RH at measures 84 and 85.

The thumb can also play on three black keys,

and on 4 white keys.

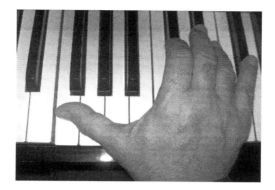

These two last instances do not appear in the standard repertoire but they can be useful in playing some of the clusters in more modern music. Another possible, though rare, use of the thumb is the simultaneous playing of two adjacent white keys and the black key between them. This can be done with the outer side of the thumb lying straight along the crack between the two white keys while the outer side of the tip of the thumb is on the black key. It can also be done by pressing the crack between the two white keys and the black one with the outer part of the cushion of the thumb, sideways and in a very extended position. The latter technique can also be used for simultaneously playing with the thumb on three adjacent white keys and the two black keys between them, but that is very rare.

Two or more fingers together on the same key

Two fingers are stronger than a single finger, can carry more weight, and endure more impact. In order to execute it we need to hold the two fingers together as if they are glued to each other, and play a little sideways, or hold the fingers one behind the other. The shorter finger usually goes behind the longer finger – closer to our body, but it can change according to the piano register we are playing, and when using this tool for chords. When either hand plays notes to the right of its own center on the keyboard, it would turn somewhat diagonally to the right; when either hand plays notes to the left of its own center on the keyboard, it would turn somewhat diagonally to the left.

The middle C is not the center of the keyboard. When we sit across the center of the keyboard, our nose would be pointing more or less at the second black key to the right of the middle C, which is the note E♭/D♯. Some people may choose to sit with their nose pointing even at the key E. Since our hands are at the sides of our body, each hand is situated across a different part of the keyboard. This is not necessarily the same part of the keyboard for every person, as it depends on the width of our body. I recommend for grownups to do most of their keyboard exercises not in the actual center of the keyboard, but away from the middle C, one octave higher for the

RH, and one octave lower for the left hand. These keyboard placements would be more or less the hands' own centers on the keyboard, and placing the hand in its own center while exercising encourages a healthier hand position.

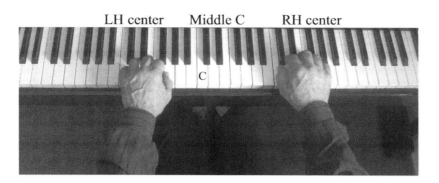

The further we go in either direction on the keyboard, the more we turn the hand, preferably with the forearm aligned (when viewed from above).

When we use the thumb together with any other finger, we do not need to play sideways as the thumb can be easily placed behind any other finger.

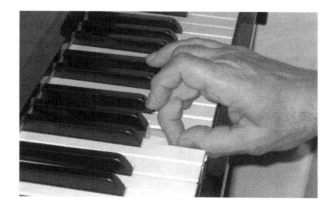

Using two fingers on one key is usually not something which is marked in the music, and therefore it does not have its own traditional way of being marked.

However, some composers/editors may still choose to mark it in the music, and they may use their own inventive markings, perhaps using a small slur, a small hairpin, or a little bracket to the side of the finger numbers, over them, or under them, or just marking two finger numbers next to a single note, above or below it, vertically or horizontally; these are partly shown in the following example. Any other inventive way may be used too.

We can also play two fingers on one key when we play two or more notes together as chords. This can help with voicing. The keys we want to sound more would be played with two fingers simultaneously.

The following G major triad in the RH will be fingered three different ways, and each fingering will bring out a different note of the triad by playing it with two fingers together. In the first chord finger 4 will be placed in front of finger 5 – closer to the fall board. In the second chord finger 2 will be placed in front of finger 3 (or behind it for playing in the lower keyboard registers). In the third chord finger 2 will be placed in front of finger 1.

It is possible to play three fingers together on a single key, black or white. Some pianists like to use fingers 3, 4, and 5 together when playing double octaves, but this is not highly recommended for hand-health reasons. The stretch and the twisted angle of the hand from the wrist can cause harm especially if played in the center area of the keyboard. This makes more sense and becomes less harmful as the LH moves towards the left end of the keyboard, and the RH moves towards the right end.

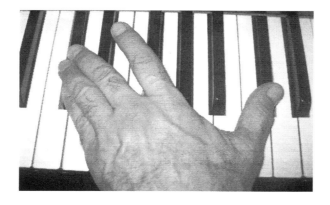

It is quite rare, but it is also possible to play together even four fingers on a single key, black or white. It can be very powerful.

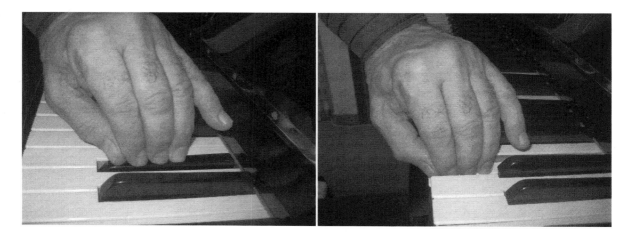

The thumb supporting other fingers

This is a variation on playing the thumb together with another finger on the same key. Instead of actually playing with both fingers, the thumb just supports the other finger by touching it somewhat firmly at the inner side of the finger anywhere between the back of the nail knuckle (the joint closest to the nail) and the back of the middle knuckle, as shown in the next two photos:

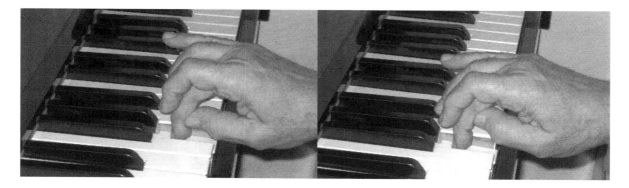

This type of support, which is similar to using two fingers on one key, is also not something which is indicated in the score, and therefore does not have a traditional marking.

Support by the hand

The fifth finger can be supported by the whole hand behind it. It has to be pretty flat and lying on its outer side, while the hand is in a vertical position, and the rest of the fingers are kept together like one unit as if glued to each other. This technique is often referred to as the "Karate Chop".

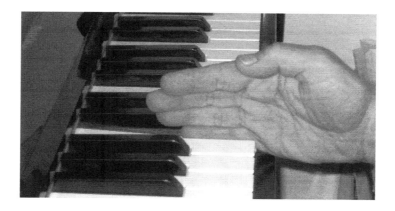

The thumb can also be supported by the whole hand. It has to be flat and placed under the hand, or more precisely under the second finger, and parallel to it, while the hand is in a normal horizontal position, and all the other fingers are flat and kept together as one unit.

Same finger on different keys

1.   This is good practice for a melody which needs to be *non-legato*, very even in sound, and very articulated. If we play every note of the melody with the same finger, it will be easier to achieve the above characteristics.

The last movement of the Saint-Saëns *Concerto No. 4 in C minor* has a RH melody which consists of single notes and is marked *sempre **ff**, marcatissimo*. This entire melody can be played with the same finger on all of the notes. Highly recommended would be finger 3, and of course due to the character of *sempre fortissimo, marcatissimo*, one may choose to support the finger with the thumb behind it. Do not attempt to work the finger from the metacarpal joint (the big knuckle between the hand and the finger – the top of the hand's arch), rather work it from the wrist as an extension of the palm.

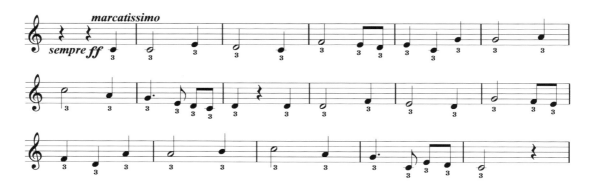

Another example is the third movement of the Bartók *Sonata*. We find Bartók's own fingering for the RH melody in measures 111 through 118, and for the LH melody in measures 119 through 126 – all thumbs (meant literally, and not in the negative sense of the expression). This fingering may seem strange, but we actually do the exact same fingering when we play this melody, or part of it, in double octaves, as then we have no choice. We do have a choice here, but the use of the same finger on the different melody notes serves a musical purpose as mentioned above. The next example shows the RH melody as it appears in measures 111-114.

2.   Repeating the same finger on different keys is also useful in double thirds and other harmonic intervals played in one hand. Repeating fingers 2\4 in the RH and 4\2 in the LH for the double thirds, can help create a *martellato* effect in *sempre fortissimo*, as Liszt uses in *Mazeppa* – the *Transcendental Etude No. 4*, from measure 7 and on.

3.   It is good practice to use the same finger on two different notes, one at the end of a phrase, and the other at the beginning of the following phrase. This fingering helps phrasing and breathing automatically and without having to give it extra attention. Let us look again at *Twinkle, Twinkle, Little Star*.

If we use the above fingering, we will get a breath between these two little phrases without having to give it any extra attention. Using finger 4 on the half note G at the end of the first phrase, and again using the same finger to start the next phrase on the quarter note F, forces us to lift it off the key G before we play the key F, thus creating a breath between these two notes. This idea of creating a breath works also when it is not necessarily the same finger playing twice successively. We can see it in the second movement of the *G major Sonata Op. 49, No. 2* by Beethoven. In measures 11-12 of this *Menuetto* Beethoven separates the ending two-note phrase G-F♯ from the previous six notes B-A-G♯-A-D♯-E, which are slurred together. Some editions make it into one phrase with no breath in between. The point here is not whether a certain interpretation is right or wrong, but how fingering can help us phrase the passage to serve our musical purpose. If we want to make sure we execute this little breath between the two slurs, we should use finger 3 on the G starting the two-note phrase G-F♯.

If we want to avoid the breath, and make it into one phrase, we should use the thumb on the G starting the two-note phrase G-F♯.

4.   After a long note, it is possible to continue to the next adjacent key with the same finger instead of the next finger, while still conveying *legato* and continuity. In the effort to help sustain the sound of a long note (which decays naturally) as long as possible, we should let the finger go off the held key only at the

very last split second, and not lift our hand off the keyboard, but move as smoothly and quickly as possible, while touching the surface of the keys, directly to the next key. Of course, the sustain pedal can help make this move even smoother. This practice also "adds a sixth finger" to our hand, and opens up more possibilities of fingering for the notes following the long note. I would like to discuss two spots in *Rondo Capriccioso Op. 14* by Mendelssohn, measures 60 and 116 of the *Presto* section. In measure 116 the RH has both melody notes in *legato* and accompaniment notes, the last of which has to be held while the melody continues. First, these melody and accompaniment notes span an interval of a seventh between F♯ and E above it, taken with fingers 2 and 5. Then, for the sake of *legato*, we would need to span the interval of a sixth between the same F♯ and D♯ above it, taken with fingers 2 and 4. Immediately following, we would need to span the interval of a fifth between the same F♯ and C♯ above it, taken with fingers 2 and 3.

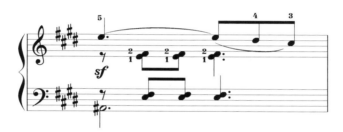

This kind of fingering causes stretches which are a little hard on the hand. This is where, after playing the long melody note with the little finger, we can continue the melody's descent using the little finger again and still convey *legato* while preserving the health of our hand.

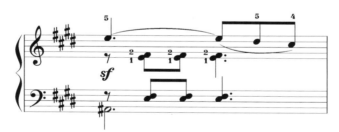

In measure 60 the LH has both melody notes in *legato* and harmony notes.

The standard fingering above poses an unpleasant stretch. I suggest that taking the melody note C with the thumb again, after it has played the previous melody note D, will not only preserve the health of the hand, but will also improve articulation of the melody that is in danger of being overpowered by the RH passages.

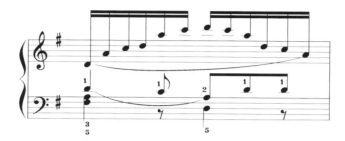

Here is another example utilizing the same idea that after a long note we can start with the same finger which played on the long note without losing continuity, thus gaining more fingering possibilities for the notes to follow. In the *Allegro moderato* (the first movement) of Beethoven's *Concerto No. 4*, measure 233 (measure 42 of the development *Solo* entrance) we have the RH playing in thirds. With the RH fingering I suggest below, not only can we do all four thirds of the sixteenths notes without having to cross fingers, we can also jump more securely from the last sixteenth using fingers 1\2 up to the next quarter note with fingers 3\5. More about the use of fingers 1\2 on a third will be discussed in "Scales in double thirds".

Repeated notes with change of fingering

We change fingering and fingers on the same repeated notes when it is necessary or when there is a reason for it. Following is a discussion of such reasons:

Reason 1. Running out of fingers. When we arrive at a key with an end finger, i.e., the little finger or the thumb, then repeat the same key, and then need to continue to another key in the same keyboard direction we have been going, we don't have another finger available in that direction (we ran out of fingers). This is when we need to change the finger on the repeated note in order to enable us to continue to play *legato* in the same direction. For example, playing *legato* the middle C going to C one octave higher, and then the same thing again but starting from that higher C at which we just arrived, we'll use RH fingers 1 and 5, then change on the repeated C from 5 to 1, and then again 5. The change of fingering on the repeated C was necessary in order to be able to play *legato* again between the thumb and finger 5 one octave higher. The LH fingering for the same is 5 and 1, then change on the repeated C from 1 to 5, and then again 1.

Let us look at this simple *Variation* on *Twinkle, Twinkle, Little Star.*

The last two quarter notes of the first measure are both G. In order to be able to continue to the next measure and play the A, we need to change fingers on the second G, thus making an extra finger available to play the A. Therefore, the repeated G is played first with finger 5, and then with finger 4. This change of fingering is necessary.

Now let us look at this same passage with the same fingering from a different angle.

What we have here, playing fingers 4 and 5 first on F and G, and then again on G and A, is a short pattern repeating itself, thus creating a sequence, which could appear over a longer span of notes in either direction of the keyboard, up or down. We can use any set of two fingers for such patterns; they can be neighboring fingers or we can skip a finger, or even two, especially if one of the fingers we use for this pattern is the thumb. Measure 147 (measure 7 of the fourth *Solo* entrance) in the first movement of Beethoven, *Concerto No. 4* is an example of a passage using such a repeated pattern. The pattern is in the RH and it starts on the fourth eighth of the measure.

Another Beethoven use of this repeated pattern is at the very beginning of the *D minor Sonata Op. 31, No. 2*, the *Tempest*. It is the *Allegro* starting in the second measure.

This sequence makes a useful exercise for each hand, up and down the keyboard, with the following various fingerings. The RH fingerings are marked above the notes and the LH fingerings are marked underneath the notes.

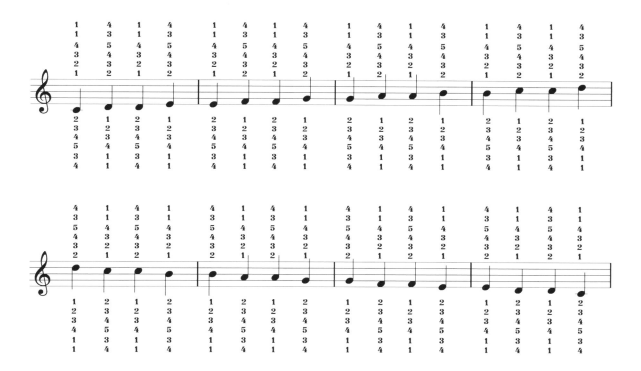

The above exercises can also be done in other keys as well as chromatically.

Related advice about technique: The above pattern is a two-note phrase. The most common technique for playing a two-note phrase is moving the wrist down while playing the first note in the phrase, and moving it back up while playing the second note. These movements do not have to be large movements, especially when playing fast. The following four photos demonstrate these movements.

Often we will also have a reason to change fingering on repeated double octaves, other harmonic intervals played in one hand, and chords (not necessarily on all the notes within the chord/interval), for similar reasons as above.

Another example is the LH in measures 12-16 of Mozart, *Sonata in F major K. 332, Allegro* (the first movement).

The patterns mentioned above can also appear in double thirds, double fourths, and other harmonic intervals played in one hand. For double thirds we can use the following pairs of fingers. RH going up: 1\3-2\4, or 2\4-1\5, or when the thumb is not available 2\4-3\5; RH going down: 2\4-1\3, or 1\5-2\4, or when the thumb is not available 3\5-2\4; LH going down: 3\1-4\2, or 4\2-5\1, or when the thumb is not available 4\2-5\3; LH going up: 4\2-3\1, or 5\1-4\2, or when the thumb is not available 5\3-4\2.

Below are suggested exercises for such patterns and sequences in double thirds. The RH fingerings are marked above the notes, and the LH fingerings are marked below the notes. These exercises can also be transposed to other keys, and can be done chromatically as well.

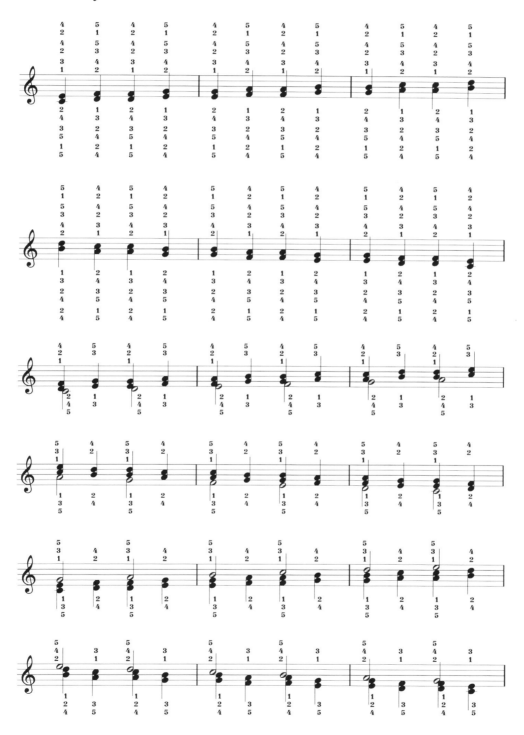

For double fourths we can use the following. RH going up: 1\4-2\5, or 2\4-1\5; RH going down: 2\5-1\4, or 1\5-2\4; LH going down: 4\1-5\2, or 4\2-5\1; LH going up: 5\2-4\1, or 5\1-4\2.

Below is a suggested exercise for such patterns and sequences in fourths. The RH fingerings are marked above the notes, and the LH fingerings are marked below the notes.

The same down and up wrist technique mentioned above is recommended for all two-note phrases, including double octaves, any other harmonic intervals played in one hand, and chords.

Reason 2. A very fast repetition of the same note. For this repetition we usually change fingers according to the number of notes in a rhythmical group, like triplets, four sixteenths, etc. For a group of two repeated notes we use fingers 1 and 2. Since skipping a finger can improve articulation and speed, using fingers 1 and 3 is a very good choice too. If possible, it is always good to use the thumb as one of the fingers in this fast repetition of the same note. When the thumb is not available, it is also possible to do the same with fingers 2 and 3; sometimes also with 3 and 4, and rarely, if at all, with fingers 4 and 5. On any of the above pairs of fingers, we can start with either finger of the pair.

The following groups of fingerings for repeated notes do not necessarily have to start on the first finger number of the group; they can start on any finger number of the group, and then just follow the order as written below, which is always a descending one in the numbering of the fingers. For a group of three repeated notes we will use fingers 3-2-1, or 4-3-2, or rarely 5-4-3. For a group of four repeated notes we will use fingers 4-3-2-1, or rarely (if the thumb is not available) 5-4-3-2. A group of five notes is quite rare, but if we need it, we will use fingers 5-4-3-2-1.

The following is an example of repeated notes in groups of two and in groups of three as they appear in the *Allegro assai* (the first movement) of Beethoven's

Sonata Op. 57 in F minor, Appassionata, measures 24-27.

Following are exercises for repeated notes with two fingerings for each hand.

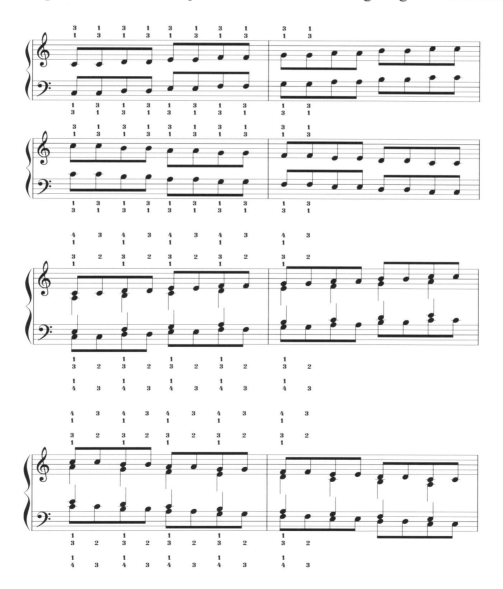

Similar exercises can also be done with chromatic scales. The following is a chromatic scale exercise for repeated notes in groups of four. This fingering can also start, should context call for it, with any finger number of the four, and continue with the same order of going to a lower finger number, though it fares better for the RH descending and the LH ascending.

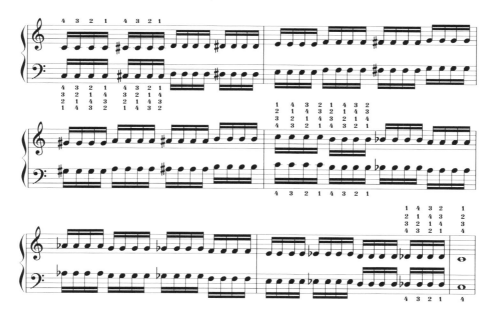

Repeated notes with no change of fingering

When there is no reason to change fingering on the same repeated notes, it is in fact undesirable to do so. Avoiding unnecessary movements improves our technique efficiency. Anyway in most cases we cannot change fingering when playing fast repeated chords, double octaves, and other harmonic intervals in one hand, as we can see in the next example. In Rachmaninov, *Concerto No. 2 in C minor*, first movement, the second *Più vivo* section has fast pairs of repeated double octaves which soon turn into fast triplets of repeated double octaves. No change of fingering occurs here.

For repeating single notes with no change of fingers we should use the same technique we use for repeating chords, double octaves, and other harmonic intervals played in one hand. We can repeat the same notes/intervals/chords/octaves in various touches, and in slower tempos we can even play them *legato* or almost *legato*. This is easier on grand pianos that have the double action feature, but also possible on other grands and uprights.

Related advice about technique: When there are fast repeated single notes played with one finger, finger 3 (or 2) is the most recommended. This helps the balance of the hand. Further help can be obtained when supporting finger 3 (or 2) with the thumb touching the inner part of the finger behind the nail knuckle.

A *legato* of the same note with the same finger is done without letting go of the key surface, similar to the use of the foot on the pedal without letting go, just moving it up and down constantly touching the pedal. A more advanced way of doing this *legato* is by partially releasing the key (not letting it return all the way up) which is similar to partially releasing the pedal.

For slow and *legato* repetition of notes we should use a small vertical wrist movement as well as a small lateral one towards or away from the fall board while slightly changing the placement of the finger on the key. If it is just two or three notes being repeated, the wrist should move a little up and inward (toward the fall board) while the finger moves slightly inward on the key.

Both hands can benefit from using this *legato* technique of repeating notes with the same finger, in the opening of Chopin's *Ballade No. 1, Op. 23 in G minor*, measures 4 and 5.

For fast repetition of notes we should use the butterfly technique: with every note the hand moves up and down from the wrist as if it is a wing of a butterfly.

For single groups of two, three, and sometimes four and even five notes/octaves/chords, the wrist moves up and inward (toward the fall board), and the finger also moves inward on the key with every note/octave/chord, while flapping the hand vertically from the wrist. These movements should be small, especially in order to allow for speed.

For prolonged fast repetition in repeated groups of two, three, and sometimes four notes/octaves/chords, as before, the wrist moves up and inward (toward the fall board), and the finger also moves inward on the key with every note in the first group. Then in the next group, the wrist moves back down and outward (away from the fall board), and the finger also moves outward with every note. All that while flapping the hand vertically from the wrist with every note.

The wrist moves a little bit in/up with each note, and a little bit out/down with each note, according to the number of notes in the group. This can be done in groups of two in/up, two out/down; three in/up, three out/down; and four in/up, four out/down. All these movements are very small and do not at all reach the highest or the lowest points of the wrist movements.

The famous Schubert song *Erlkönig* has in the RH repeated double octaves in groups of three notes which can benefit a lot from using the above technique.

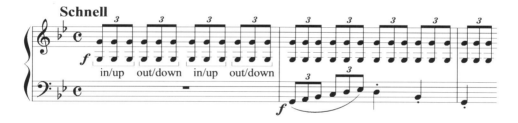

Towards the end of the Liszt, *Concert Paraphrase* on *Rigoletto* by Verdi, there are repeated double octaves in groups of two and of four. The groups of four can be played with movements of 4-note groups or be divided into 2-note groups and played accordingly. They can also be played with movements of 4-note groups that start on 2-note groups and continue to the first two notes of the following 4-note groups. The following examples show three different ways of moving the RH for measure 78:

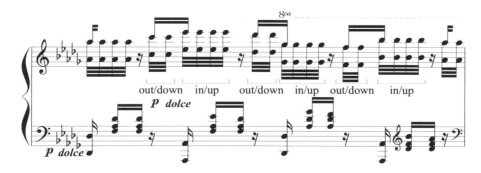

The wrist movements of in/up and out/down over the keys, which are done according to the number of notes in the group, do not necessarily have to be grouped according to the rhythmic grouping. The movements can have their own grouping sequences starting on any note of the group, the first, the second, the third, etc.

The next example is taken from Beethoven's *Appassionata*, first movement, measure 8 of the recapitulation section. The LH shows a set of repeated harmonic intervals grouped in three eighths. The wrist movements of in/up and out/down are better done here starting from the second note of each group. This will complement shaping the musical phrase from the second note in the group into the first note of the next group.

The RH in *Erlkönig* can also be executed in this manner, should one choose to shape the phrase here in this way.

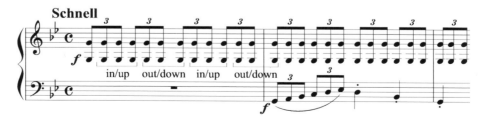

The thumb as a pivot

As a rule (of thumb...), using the thumb like a pivot between other fingers can be very useful and helpful. In many instances the thumb can replace finger 3 and be used as a pivot between fingers 2 and 4 for better articulation, clarity, and evenness. The thumb can also be used as a pivot between fingers 2 and 3, and between fingers 3 and 4. A pivoting thumb is particularly useful in a *gruppetto* (a five-note turn, or its shorter version containing four notes, which is marked in the music with a symbol similar to the tilde mark: "∞"), and in ornamented beginnings and endings of trills, such as *vorschlag* and *nachschlag*.

The RH figuration in the very beginning of Mozart's *Rondo Alla Turca* from the *Sonata in A major K. 331* is a four-note *gruppetto* which can be fingered in different ways. Following is my favorite fingering, where for the first and third *gruppettos* I use thumb pivoting, and for the second, fourth, and fifth *gruppettos* I use straightforward five-finger position fingering. Although the fingering of 3-1-2-1 could be used here for every *gruppetto*, it fits the hand better when finger 2 falls on a black key. However the transition from the third *gruppetto* to the fourth one is executed better if we don't have to make the leap to finger 3 on B and immediately also have the thumb on A.

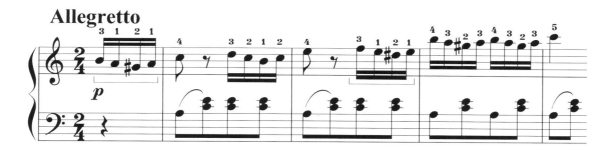

The next example is from the *Vivace* (the first movement) of the Haydn *D major Concerto*, measures 24-25 in the first *Solo* entrance. The RH thumb serves twice as a pivot between fingers 3 and 4, and then at the end of the passage between fingers 3 and 2.

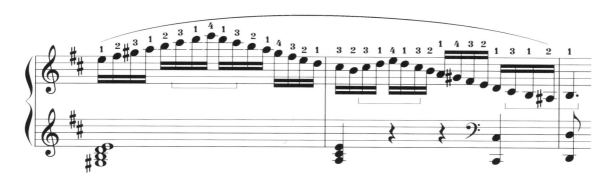

In the second measure of the Chopin's *Nocturne Op. 9, No. 2* the RH thumb serves as a pivot between fingers 3 and 2.

A classic example of a pivotal thumb is of course the RH in Chopin's *Étude Op. 25, No. 2*. The next example shows my fingering suggestion for the first measure.

The theme of the *Rondo* (the third movement) in Beethoven, *Concerto No. 4, Op. 58* has a series of short trills in the RH, each ending with a *nachschlag*. The thumb, serving as a pivot between fingers 4 and 2, can be very useful here, and the same fingering can be repeated for all five trills in measures 5-8 of the first *Solo*.

As this fingering can become a nice habit, I would advise to try and avoid using the same finger on both sides of the pivoting thumb as much as possible, and especially in fast tempos.

For example, in measure 15 of the Chopin *Prelude Op. 28, No. 16* the last six sixteenth notes in the RH would be fingered better with 4-3-2-1-3-2 rather than 5-4-3-2-1-2. Ending with 2-1-2, as suggested in some editions, is not a very good idea at this speed, even more so because the first note in the next measure is the thumb again.

Should you want to play the top E flat with finger 5, it would be better to cross to finger 3 after the thumb plays on E natural and then use finger 2 on C. This will result in the following fingering: 5-4-3-2-1-3-2. As may be deduced from the above fingering suggestion, and along the same lines, I would also advise to try and avoid using the thumb on both sides of any other pivoting finger.

In measure 16 of the Chopin *Waltz No. 14, Op. Posthumous in E minor* the RH would be fingered better with 5-3-2-1-4-2-1 rather than 5-3-2-1-2-1-2 or 5-4-3-2-1-2-1, as suggested in some editions.

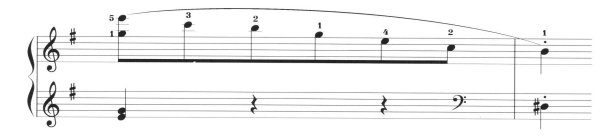

All that said, I do recommend the following exercises for crossing and pivoting. Play the C major scale using only two fingers such as 1-2, or 1-3, or 1-4.

Related advice about technique: Applying the forearm rotation technique, in which the weight is shifted from side to side, will help execute pivotal fingering as well as any other fingering for turns and trills.

Thumb crawling

This might be one of my own inventions. You can crawl with your thumb from a white key to an adjacent one, white or black, in *legato* playing. You can also crawl with your thumb from one black key to an adjacent one; this is best done in the direction of RH descending and LH ascending. This may rarely be called for, but is possible and useful should the other fingers be occupied holding or playing other notes, or when playing double octaves. Obviously we don't need this technique for moving from a black key to the adjacent white one as that is done by simple finger sliding. In order to execute thumb crawling between two white keys or two black keys you need to use the outer side of the nail knuckle in addition to the outer side of the tip of your thumb. For executing it between white and black keys you need to use the outer side of the hand knuckle too.

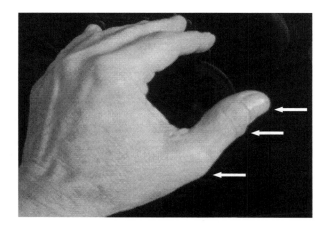

Outer side of tip of thumb

Outer side of nail knuckle

Outer side of hand knuckle

Thumb crawling between two white keys or between two black keys: After playing a key with your thumb, on the same playing spot, and while lowering your wrist, you slide from the outer side of the tip of your thumb to the outer side of the nail knuckle, which would cause the tip of your thumb to be raised a little in the air. Now point the tip of your thumb in the direction you are going, and it will already be practically over and touching the next key you are about to play (the three photos below show different examples of the thumb tip being raised over the next key). Then just play the next key with the tip of your thumb while raising your wrist.

Thumb crawling from white to black keys: Repeat the steps described in the previous paragraph with the exception of sliding from the tip of your thumb all the way to the outer side of the hand knuckle, rather than just to the nail knuckle, as shown in the next two photos.

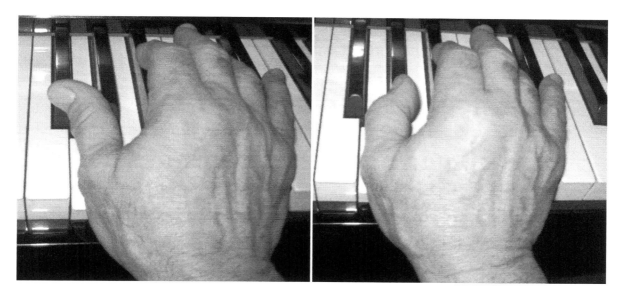

Two examples of where this crawling thumb *legato* can be used in playing double octaves are found in the *Rigoletto Concert Paraphrase* by Liszt. One spot is at the end of measure 2, where a RH double octave (A♮) descends from white to black keys (G♯).

Another spot is 10 measures from the end of the piece, the measure before *Presto*. At the end of this measure the RH has a double octave on a black key (E♭ marked with a *fermata*) descending to another double octave on a black key (D♭).

A reversed technique for thumb crawling can also be used when moving from a white key to another one regardless of whether it is black or white. RH descending and LH ascending: after you play the first white key, raise your wrist a little and curve your thumb so the nail knuckle is over the next white key (next photo on the left). Now just play that key with your nail knuckle while lowering your wrist. RH ascending and LH descending: after you play the first white key, raise your wrist a little and extend your thumb so the nail knuckle is over the next white key (next photo on the right). Now just play that key with your nail knuckle while lowering your wrist. For moving the same way to a black key, start with the thumb playing on the white key much closer to the fall board so it is placed between the black keys.

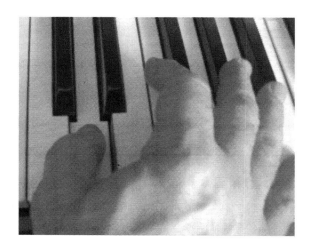 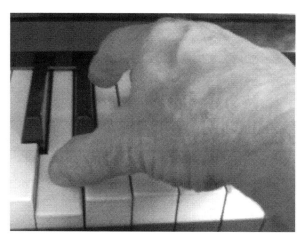

Playing a scale of white keys and continuously alternating between these two techniques would thus resemble the heel-toe foot technique of playing the organ pedals.

Skipping a finger – trills and turns

Although the traditional five-finger position teaches us to use consecutive fingers for consecutive keys, skipping a finger in playing two neighboring keys can improve our agility and articulation. This is very useful in trills and turns; on occasion, it can also be used in scales and in parts of scales.

Trilling with fingers 1 and 3, instead of with fingers 2 and 3 or 1 and 2, is a common practice for pianists. I often trill also with fingers 1 and 4, as was shown above in the example of the theme from the *Rondo* in Beethoven, *Concerto No. 4*.

Another common practice in trills is alternating fingers. This practice of fingering a trill would most commonly use the following fingering succession: 1-3-2-3 which combines both ideas of using neighboring fingers and skipping a finger. Though not much in use, the curious pianist may want to experiment with the following various sets of alternating fingers in trills: 1-4-2-4, 1-3-1-2, 1-4-1-2, 1-4-1-3, and 1-4-2-3.

A trill with crossed fingers may also be useful on occasion, though perhaps not too often. In such a case, trilling with fingers 1 and 3 while they are crossed would most likely be the best. Trilling with crossed fingers means that if, for example, we trill in the RH between the notes E♭ and F (best to try in the middle of the keyboard) we would put finger 3 on E♭ and finger 1 on F.

An example of how we can use a trill with crossed fingers is found at the end of Chopin, *Polonaise in A♭ major Op. 53*. Eleven measures before the end, the RH has a trill on E♭ which can be taken with fingers 3 and the thumb while being crossed. This enables us to play the following D with finger 2 as well as to have a more powerful grip of the trill with a better balanced and healthier hand/arm angle that keeps the elbow at a little distance from the body. Revealing my own little secrets which are not shown in the next example, I actually play the E♭ of the trill with fingers 2 and 3 together. I also take with the LH thumb the D that follows the trill, thus adding it to the diminished chord of the LH as the top note; this happens to be an example of using the Redistribution tool which will be discussed later on. This example also shows another fingering tool that is discussed later on: the crossing between fingers 1 and 5, or 5 and 1.

Trilling with fingers 2 and 4 would be an improvement over trilling with fingers 3 and 4; it could also be an improvement over trilling with fingers 2 and 3.

When it is necessary to free fingers 1 and 2 for playing or holding other notes at the same time, and where it is applicable, trilling with fingers 3 and 5, can also provide a better execution than trilling with 4 and 5 or 3 and 4. Cases like these can be found often in Bach, Beethoven, and other composers.

The next example is measure 4 in Bach, *Prelude No. 4, WTC, Book I*. The RH has to trill the notes D♯ and E while holding the notes G♯ and B♯ below the trill. The number of times that fingers 5 and 3 are written repeatedly in the trill is not intended to indicate how long or dense the trill should be.

Another example is measure 4 in Bach, *Prelude No. 12, Book 1*, where the RH has to trill the notes B♭ and C while playing and holding the note D♭ below the trill. Here too, the number of times that fingers 5 and 3 are written repeatedly in the trill is not intended to indicate how long or dense the trill should be.

The next example is Beethoven, *Sonata No. 8 in C minor, Op. 13, Pathétique*. In measures 38-39 of the *Allegro molto e con brio* (after the second *Grave*) the RH has a trill on E♭ while playing and holding C a third below. The trill ends with a *nachschlag* leading to D and B a third below. This situation requires finger 3 on the E♭, and it enables us to use fingers 3 and 5 for the trill.

Another Beethoven example is the long RH trills towards the end of the last *Sonata, Op. 111 in C minor*. While trilling the top G, the melody has to be played below the trill with the same hand. The melody is best done with the thumb; naturally, the use of the sustain pedal is quite desirable here. Following are measures 16-17 from the end. The number of times that fingers 5 and 3 are written repeatedly in the trill does not suggest how long or dense the trill should be.

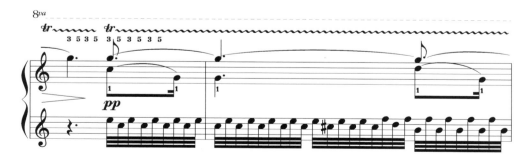

Mordents and other turns can also be executed with more clarity when we skip a finger or sometimes even two.

The mordent-like motif in the *Presto* of *Rondo Capriccioso Op. 14* by Mendelssohn can benefit from it wherever possible, particularly in the RH. The next example shows the beginning of the *Presto* with fingers 5-3-5 in the RH.

Related advice about technique: In prolonged trills, i.e., longer than three measures of four beats in *Allegro*, it would be helpful to change fingerings, if possible, as you go along while the trill lasts in order to prevent repetitive strain injury.

Crossing fingers, other than the thumb

Older than thumb crossing, this technique follows the idea of "paired fingerings" used in the very old school of the 16th century when the thumb and the little finger were not used at all for keyboard playing. This technique is very useful and in many cases absolutely necessary. Usually, we will pass a lower finger number over a higher one when ascending in the RH and descending in the LH as shown in the next photo on the left. The opposite directions, which are RH descending and LH ascending, will usually have a higher finger number passing under a smaller one as shown in the photo on the right.

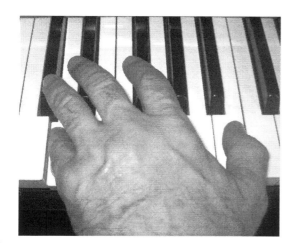

This technique is particularly important when the thumb, and sometimes also finger 2 of the same hand, are busy playing or holding other notes.

The next example shows the RH thumb playing and holding the middle C and the LH thumb playing and holding the E below while the other fingers play a line above and below the held notes, respectively. The lines played by the other fingers require such non-thumb finger crossing. Two fingering possibilities are shown in this example which can also be used as an exercise and is not necessarily meant to be played hands together.

This type of crossing does not work well if we want to cross a lower finger number over a higher one from a black key to a white key ascending in the RH and descending in the LH. It also doesn't work well when crossing a higher finger number under a lower one from a white key to a black key descending in the RH and ascending in the LH. Therefore, the next example/exercise, in which both hands are playing and holding two notes with the thumb and finger 2, shows only one fingering possibility. Unlike the previous example, here it would not be a good idea to use finger 3 on G in the RH and on A in the LH, in both the first and second measures, as it would make this type of crossing even more awkward and more uncomfortable than it already is.

Preludes and Fugues by Bach often call for this type of crossing, especially when one desires a perfect *legato* articulation without the use of the sustain pedal.

The famous Chopin *Étude Op. 10, No. 2* is a classic example of a piece which calls for this technique and which was actually written for the purpose of learning and practicing it. Here is the first measure.

Legato scales of double octaves, double thirds, and other harmonic intervals played in one hand will require these tricky crossings, as will be discussed in their respective sections of the book ahead.

Unlike the previously discussed hand position for regular scales and arpeggios, where the wrists and the elbows point outwards with the little finger sides of the hands raised, this type of crossing requires the opposite hand position. Here the crossing can be facilitated by the hand being slightly collapsed at the side of the little finger and the wrist pointing somewhat inward, which means that the hand points a little outwards. All that is done while the elbow stays closer to the side of the body, depending of course on the keyboard register being played.

Suggested exercises: Play a two octave scale using only fingers 4-5, 3-4, and 2-3. The following exercises are best done hands separately.

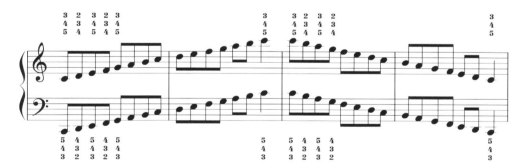

Then play a two octave scale with fingers 3-4-5, and 2-3-4.

Finally, play a two octave scale with fingers 2-3-4-5.

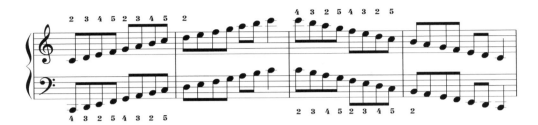

Now let us do the exercises above also with an added note in the thumb of each hand. The first and second exercises have six different sets of fingerings for each hand. The third exercise has four sets of fingerings for each hand.

Here is an exercise with two added notes. Each hand has two different fingerings.

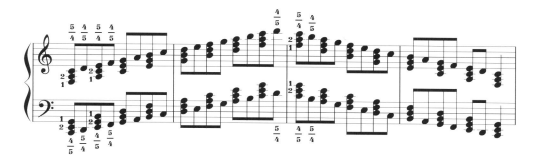

The last exercise in this series is a chromatic one.

Crossing and shifting between fingers 1 and 5

While crossing is a *legato* move which enables us to get from one hand position to another, shifting is a *non-legato* move which enables us to get from one hand position to another. We usually employ the technique of shifting for positions which are further apart where we cannot do a proper *legato* crossing. We can cross and shift, both in scales and in arpeggios, between any finger and the thumb. Doing so between fingers 5 and 1 might be a less-popular move, but it is nonetheless an important tool which was favored by Chopin and Liszt.

Sometimes we do not have any other choice of fingering, like in the RH passages at 8 and at 12 measures before the end of *Prelude No. 24* from *Op. 28* by Chopin. This passage repeats a descending five-note pattern F-E-D-B-G in four descending octaves, and the only efficient way to finger it in this fast tempo is 5-4-3-2-1, and then cross/shift from finger 1 to 5, and again use 5-4-3-2-1, etc.

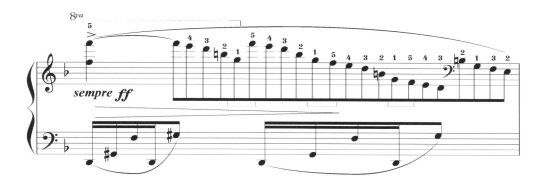

Also in Chopin's *Impromptu No. 1 in A♭ major, Op.* 29, measure 47 of the middle section, there is practically no other choice of efficient fingering for the RH but to repeatedly use 5-4-3-2-1, and cross/shift between fingers 1 and 5.

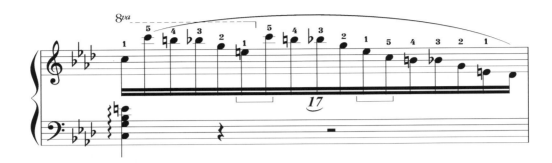

Another such example is in Brahms, *Concerto No. 2 in B♭ major, Op. 83*, at 65 measures before the end of the *Allegro non troppo* (the first movement). Both hands play the same passage one octave apart. The passage consists of five ascending notes (F, A, C, D, and E♭), repeated three times in three ascending octaves. The standard fingering for this very fast passage is: RH 1-2-3-4-5, then cross/shift to finger 1, etc.; LH 5-4-3-2-1, then cross/shift to finger 5, etc. We can also use the thumb on A in either hand, however, crossing/shifting between fingers 1 and 5 remains inevitable.

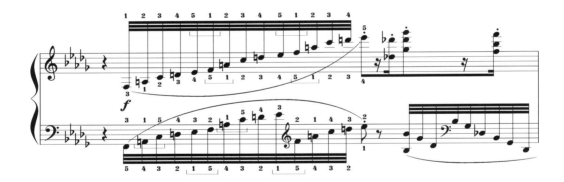

But even when there is a choice of other fingerings, sometimes choosing and using this tool can improve articulation or speed, depending on the case, as well as protect the hand from injury. An example would be an ascending two octave arpeggio of the C major 7th chord starting with the RH on the middle C. The notes are C-E-G-B-C-E-G-B. I would definitely consider using finger 5 on the B instead of the traditional finger 4. If it was a B♭, I would be inclined to use the traditional finger 4. But, on B♮, I believe that using finger 5 can give a better grip, security, and articulation. As important, it would also prove much healthier for the hand by preventing that uncomfortable stretch between fingers 3 and 4 along with the bad twist of the hand to the right. The same C major 7th arpeggio passage in the LH would also benefit from this fingering tool. The next example shows both hands.

Following are a few examples in which I would recommend using fingers 1-2-3-5 rather than 1-2-3-4. Chopin, *Polonaise in A♭ Major Op. 53*, measure 52:

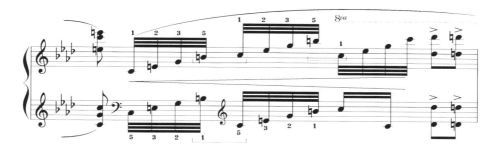

Chopin, *Étude in Cm Op. 10*, *No. 12*, the LH in measure 40:

Chopin, *Étude in Fm Op. 25*, *No. 2*, the RH, seven measures before the end:

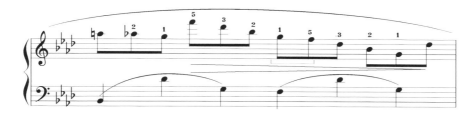

Beethoven, *Concerto No. 4*, first movement, the LH in measure 9 of the second *Solo* (the same fingering is also applicable two measures later):

Alternative fingerings for some scales

Fingering, and scale fingering in particular, can be divided into two groups:

1.   Fingering which is mentally more comfortable, e.g., because it is consistent, as in some pattern fingering, or because it is parallel, as in the traditional fingering of the C major scale when the two hands play together in contrary motion.

2.   Fingering which is mentally less comfortable, e.g., the traditional fingering of the C major scale when both hands play together in a parallel motion.

It is important to note that sometimes the less comfortable fingering for the mind may be the better fingering for the music and for the well-being of the hands. Though they have their merits, I do not consider fingering consistency and other fingering types that make the thinking job easy a first priority. As a matter of fact, the order of my priorities is:

1.   Musical consideration.
2.   Health of the hands.
3.   Making it physically easy and comfortable.
4.   Making it mentally easy and comfortable.

While some scales have fixed and quite-unchangeable traditional fingerings, some others can benefit, at times, from alternative fingerings too. The scales with all five black keys have fixed fingerings which would be changed very rarely. The scales with fewer black keys can be played with alternative fingerings as necessary. C major, which is all white keys, can naturally be played with the most variety of alternative fingerings. The use of alternative fingerings would depend on a number of factors: desired type of execution, length of passage, passage points of beginning and end, changes of pitch direction (up and down on the keyboard) and their points of change, skipping or repeating notes in the scale, musical context that precedes or follows the scale, and how we get into and out of the scale.

Crossing/shifting between fingers 1 and 5 is a great tool here too. Consider an ascending two-octave C major scale with the RH starting from the middle C. For the fastest execution use fingers 1 through 5 three times in succession. The five-finger position on five consecutive notes can be blocked and played as a chord. I often joke saying that one cannot get any faster than playing the five notes together. For real speed, the blocked five-note groups should be played like three fast-rolled chords. Using the traditional fingering in this two-octave scale, we have to cross the thumb three times; the suggested alternative fingering has only two crossings instead of three. As finger crossing slows us down, this would allow for a much faster execution. This fingering tool may not be appropriate for the music styles of Bach and Mozart, as they themselves did not use it. Beethoven may be a borderline case regarding the use of this fingering tool, but from Chopin and Liszt onwards, it can be very appropriate. As a matter of fact, Liszt was very fond of this fingering.

In the *Allegro con brio, ma non leggiere* (the third movement) of Prokofiev, *Sonata No. 4, Op. 29*, the very opening scale passage and similar scale passages towards the end of the movement could use the type of scale fingering suggested above. If we alternate between the hands all the way through, we do not need the fingering suggested above, but if, at a high speed, we are concerned about getting the left hand to the next bass note/octave in time, this fingering can be very useful. The following example is 17 measures from the end of the *Sonata*, and it will show the last of these passages which is also the longest one of the lot.

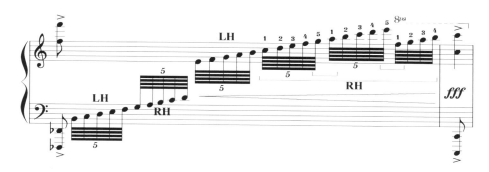

Of course, some pianists may like to play it as a *glissando* instead of a played out scale. It is possible to do it as a *glissando*, but it does present a little problem of getting smoothly and with no gap from the last note of the *glissando* to the octave that follows.

In Prokofiev's *Concerto No. 1, Op. 10*, measures 65-66 of the first movement, this type of fingering is put to good use.

Suppose we want to play the C major scale, either hand in either direction, producing a very decisive *forte* sound. In this case I would suggest using just fingers 1, 2, and 3, repeatedly, as they are our strongest fingers.

The next example shows such a scale in the second measure of the *Prelude* from the Bach/Busoni *Toccata in C major, BWV 564*.

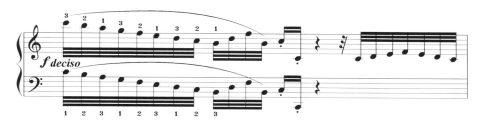

In fact, this type of fingering appears as indicated by the composer in *urtext* editions of Beethoven's last *Sonata, Op. 111*, four measures before the very end.

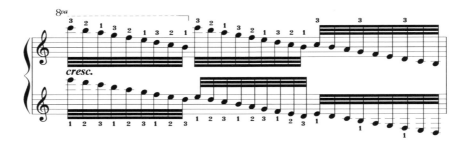

Another example of a passage in which this fingering idea can be useful is measures 15 and 17 in the third movement of Beethoven's *Concerto No. 1*. Following are the right hand scales in measures 15-17:

This fingering idea can also help rhythm, evenness, articulation, accentuation, and phrasing, when applied to scales actually written in groups of three notes. Following are two examples from Beethoven's *Sonata No. 20, Op. 49, No. 2*, first movement. The LH in measure 44 (also repeated an octave lower in measure 47):

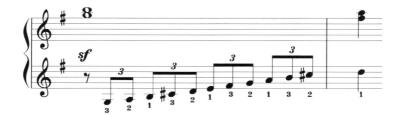

The RH in measures 9, 11, and 13 of the recapitulation section:

Often, using F major/minor fingering in the RH (1-2-3-4-1-2-3-4) and B major/minor fingering in the LH (4-3-2-1-4-3-2-1) for C major/minor and other similar scales in either direction, can prove very useful too. In many cases using this fingering will enhance strength, evenness of notes, and equal shaping of phrases in general. The earlier example of measures 15 and 17 in the third movement of Beethoven's *Concerto No. 1* can serve us here too; this time by using the F major fingering for the RH, which is two groups of the fingers 1-2-3-4. We do not necessarily have to start on the first finger of the group. Therefore, the following RH scales in measures 15-17 show three fingering possibility, all in four-finger groups.

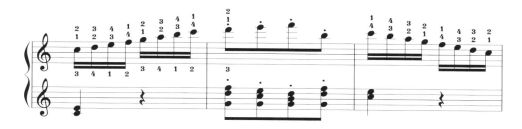

In the following example this fingering idea will also help to subdivide the phrases in a musical way by shaping them equally from the second sixteenth in the beat to the first sixteenth in the next beat.

Beethoven, *Sonata Op. 49, No. 2*, the *Minuet* (the second movement), measures 21-22 and measures 25-26:

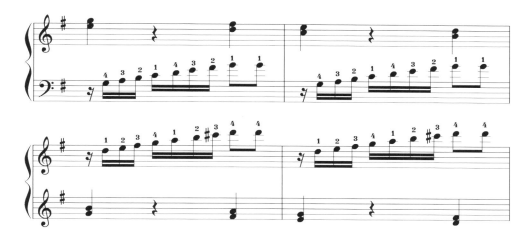

Another similar case is the LH in Mozart, *Sonata in C major K. 545*, first movement, third and fourth measures in the development section.

There is an interesting passage starting 16 measures before the *Cadenza* of the first movement in Beethoven's *Concerto No. 3*. We often find in Beethoven scale passages with different rhythmical groups of notes, such as this two-measure long descending scale. It consists of five-note, four-note, and three-note groups. It could be interesting to finger the groups of notes with their parallel groups of fingers. We can work out this fingering backwards by placing the thumb at the end of every such group of notes. As a result, the five-note groups start with finger 5, the four-note groups start with finger 4, and the three-note groups start with finger 3.

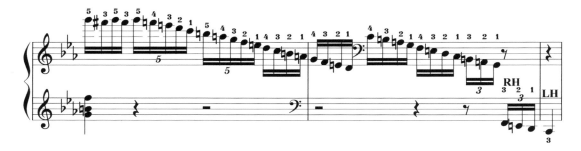

Using, in scales, fingers 1 and 4 successively instead of fingers 4 and 5 at top ends and turning points for the RH, and at bottom ends and turning points for the LH, is also a handy tool. We already discussed the same in "The thumb as a pivot", where it was introduced as the thumb pivoting between fingers 3 and 4. Another part of the Haydn *D major Concerto* will exemplify the same idea. This part is in the first movement, two measures before the *Tutti* recapitulation.

Here is an example in the LH. Mozart, *A major Concerto K. 488*, third movement, the four-bar passage starting 23 measures before the end of the piece:

A similar idea would be to use, in scales, finger 1 instead of finger 4 at top ends and turning points for the RH, and at bottom ends and turning points for LH.

Let us look at the RH of the same passage from the third movement of Mozart's *A major Concerto K. 488*.

Along the same lines, another similar idea would be to use, in scales, finger 1 instead of finger 5 at top ends and turning points for the RH, and at bottom ends and turning points for the LH. It is like the traditional fingering of a RH ascending and a LH descending C major scale when crossing the thumb for the start of a second octave, except that here we do not continue to play the second octave; we either stop, or turn back. The next example is from Mozart, *Sonata in F major, K. 332*, third movement, measure 32 in the recapitulation.

Another example is from *Rondo all' Ongharese* of the Haydn *D major Concerto*, 20 measures before the end of the piece.

Yet another handy tool for scales is skipping the fourth finger, and using finger 5 instead, at top ends and turning points for the RH, and at bottom ends and turning points for the LH. Once again let us look at the same RH passage from the Mozart *A major Concerto K. 488*, third movement, the four-bar passage starting 23 measures before the end of the piece. This time it is with a different fingering than before in order to show this particular fingering possibility.

Here is an example for the LH from the *Rondo* of Beethoven, *Concerto No. 4.* Measures 45-48.

Suggested exercises: Play two-octave scales, both directions in each hand, using each of the following groups of fingers in succession: 1-2-3, 1-3-4, 1-4-5, 1-2-3-4, 1-3-4-5, 1-2-3-4-5.

As mentioned before, traditional scale fingerings are created by using the two groups of fingers: 1-2-3 and 1-2-3-4. Various nontraditional fingerings can be created by starting either of the two groups not on their first finger, a practice used also in some traditional scale fingerings. Additionally, some traditional scale fingerings can become nontraditional if used for scales that traditionally do not employ them.

Traditional fingerings of harmonic minor scales often require an unpleasant stretch between the RH fingers 3 and 4 for the augmented second which is a step and a half (three semitones). Using the RH F major/minor fingering 1-2-3-4-1-2-3-4 for the harmonic minor scales A, E, D, G, and C, will solve this problem, and the stretch will be between fingers 2 and 3, which is much more tolerable. However in order to avoid any stretch whatsoever, I suggest, for the same scales mentioned above, the following fingering: 1-2-3-4-1-2-4-5. The B minor harmonic scale can benefit from this stretch-free fingering for the RH: 3-4-1-2-3-1-2-3.

The B♭ minor harmonic scale can benefit from the following stretch-free fingering for the RH, but only for strong and articulated results, not for very high speeds: 3-1-2-3-1-3-1-3. We can gain somewhat more speed with no stretch if we use the traditional fingering with one alteration of using the thumb instead of finger 3 on A, thus: 4-1-2-3-1-2-1-4.

The harmonic minor scales of A, E, and B can also benefit from another stretch-free fingering for the RH, which is the traditional fingering for the harmonic minor scales F♯, C♯, and G♯: 3-4-1-2-3-1-2-3.

The RH in C minor harmonic can also use this stretch-free fingering, which can be used for F♯ minor too: 2-3-4-1-2-3-1-2.

Stretching fingers 3-4 over a whole step where one of the keys is black and the other is white, can also be unpleasant for some people. Some alternative scale fingerings can help us avoid that as well. The RH in D minor natural can benefit from this completely stretch-free fingering: 2-3-1-2-3-4-1-2.

The LH stretch, between fingers 2 and 3 in the traditional fingering, is the more tolerable one. However, an alternative fingering can completely eliminate any stretch here as well.

The LH in the harmonic minor scales A, E, D, G, C, and F, can be played with the fingering 5-4-3-2-1-4-2-1. The harmonic minor scales A, E, and B can be played with the fingering 3-2-1-3-2-1-4-3. The latter can also be used for the harmonic minor scales F♯, C♯, and G♯, but it is not necessary because the traditional fingering is already stretch-free. The LH in C minor harmonic can also be played with 4-3-2-1-3-2-1-4.

The LH in A minor natural and harmonic, D minor melodic, and D major can also be played with the fingering of D♯ minor: 2-1-4-3-2-1-3-2. In addition, D major and D minor melodic can be played with the fingering 2-1-3-2-1-4-3-2, though I personally like it less due to the slight stretch of fingers 4-3 over B-C♯. The same goes for playing F major with this alternative fingering: 3-2-1-4-3-2-1-3. When possible, I would rather avoid even the smallest stretch, such as between fingers 4-3 playing Bb-C.

B♭ minor harmonic can be played with the following stretch-free fingering for the LH, but only for strong and articulated results, not for very high speeds: 3-1-3-2-1-3-1-3. We can gain somewhat more speed with no stretch if we use the traditional fingering with one alteration of using the thumb instead of finger 3 on A, thus: 2-1-3-2-1-4-1-2.

One more exercise suggestion for the road: even though this may seem a bit awkward, it could prove a useful exercise to practice in both hands all scales, arpeggios, and dominant 7th arpeggios, using the traditional fingerings of C major scale, arpeggio, and dominant 7th arpeggio. For example, play the C♯ major scale with the RH fingering 1-2-3-1-2-3-4-5 and the LH fingering 5-4-3-2-1-3-2-1. As mentioned before, comfort is not necessarily a first priority, and this exercise will help immensely in developing the technique.

Chromatic scales

The traditional fingering will give us the most articulation: finger 3 on the black keys; finger 1 on the single white keys D, G, and A; fingers 1 and 2 on the two pairs of white keys E-F and B-C.

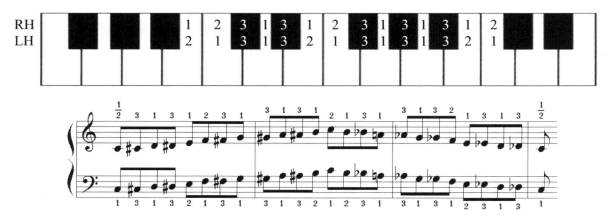

However, for utmost speed we should reduce the number of thumb crossings as shown in the next example. To illustrate this, we will start with the RH finger 1 on E going up, and the LH finger 1 on C going down: 1-2-3-1-2-3-4-1-2-3-4-5-1…

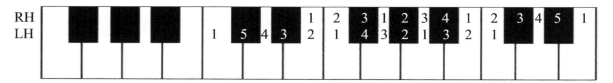

Like in playing very fast scales with the alternative fingering that uses crossing between the thumb and the little finger, this fingering tool may not be appropriate for the music styles of Bach and Mozart, but it can be very appropriate for the music styles of Chopin, Liszt, and onwards.

Often, pianists will also use a combination of the two chromatic scale fingering types mentioned above. To illustrate this, we will start with the RH finger 1 on E going up, and the LH finger 1 on C going down: 1-2-3-1-2-3-4-1-2-3-1-3-1…

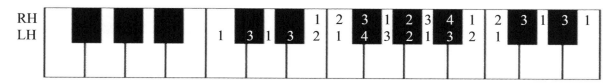

Of course, one can make even further variations on these chromatic scale fingerings. One of my personal variations on the traditional chromatic fingering is using RH finger 4 on A♯ and sometimes also on D♯, and LH finger 4 on G♭ and sometimes also on Db. Thus, C to C ascending chromatic scale in the RH, and E to E descending chromatic scale in the LH can also be played with this fingering: 2-3-1-4-1-2-3-1-3-1-4-1-2.

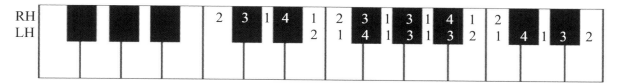

Another small variation on the last fingering would be to use the RH finger 4 on D♯ and on G♯, and the LH finger 4 on Db and on Ab. Thus, C to C ascending chromatic scale in the RH and E to E descending chromatic scale in the LH can also be played with this fingering: 2-3-1-4-1-2-3-1-4-1-3-1-2. This variation follows the idea of not using the same finger on both sides of a pivoting thumb. This last fingering variation can serve all purposes: agility, smoothness, and articulation.

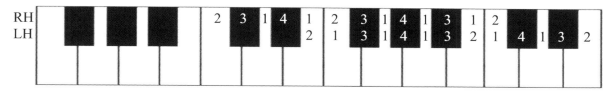

In measure 27 of the *Ab major Waltz, Op. 69, No. 1* by Chopin, there is a RH ascending chromatic scale passage that contains 14 notes, including the *gruppetto* at the beginning of the passage. This passage appears three times identically, but the musician within the piano player may want to render it differently every time. I chose three different fingerings to do the musical job for me. The following example will show four different fingering possibilities, each enabling a somewhat different interpretation. The first possibility, the one right on top of the notes, is the most articulated one. The second possibility, the one above the first possibility, starts with the same articulation as the first one, but immediately changes into a more smooth and elegant flow of the passage. The third possibility is smooth and elegant all the way through. The fourth possibility is probably even smoother than the third one.

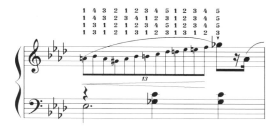

It is interesting to note that very articulated, even, and precise playing often gives the impression of being faster than it actually is.

Correlation between simultaneous fingerings in both hands

Finding connections between simultaneous fingerings in both hands is mentally comfortable. The more linkage there is, the easier it is for our mind. As mentioned previously, playing the traditional fingering of the C major scale, two hands together in contrary motion, would be a very comfortable task for the mind. The thinking is symmetric, the fingering is parallel, every finger in one hand mirrors the same finger in the other hand, and they play at the same time.

This parallel fingering idea can sometimes be kept and used even if the mirroring image is not a perfect one.

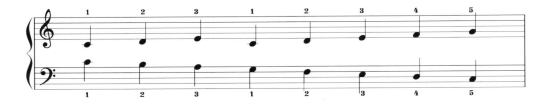

But, what happens when we play the C major scale in parallel motion, where the symmetry is of the notes and of the keys, but not of the fingering? Is there no fingering correlation here at all? Actually there is: fingers 3 in both hands always play together.

If we can find such connections in our fingering, it will make many things easier for the mind. If we can create such fingering, and at the same time make it suit the musical character we desire, preserve the health of the hands, and be physically comfortable, we will have achieved the ideal fingering.

Let us try to check such reciprocal fingerings in various parallel motion passages of the two hands playing together. Playing a pentascale with the five-finger position obviously gives us finger 3 in both hands always together. In addition, the thumb in one hand is always together with the little finger in the other hand, and finger 4 in one hand is always together with finger 2 in the other hand.

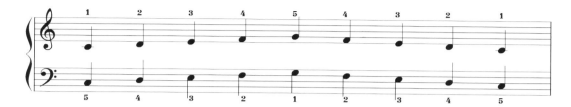

As derived from the "General rule" of scale fingering, scales with all five black keys, such as F♯ major, C♯ major, C♯ minor melodic, B♭ minor natural, and E♭ minor natural, share the following:

1. The thumbs are always together and on white keys.
2. The group of fingers 2-3 in one hand mirrors the group of fingers 3-2 in the other hand and is always on the group of two black keys.
3. The group of fingers 2-3-4 in one hand mirrors the group of fingers 4-3-2 in the other hand and is always on the group of three black keys.

C♯ major: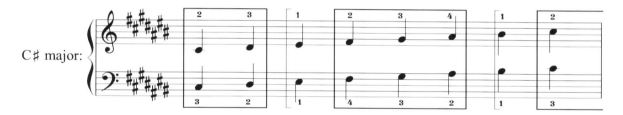

B major has similar characteristics to the above group of scales as well. The only difference is that the first note of the first octave in the LH is played with finger 4, and the last note of the last octave in the RH is played with finger 5. Actually, it is the thumb that is supposed to be used on the note B in the two cases described above, and fingers 4 and 5, respectively, are used in order to prevent an extra and unnecessary thumb crossing.

The harmonic and melodic forms of the B♭ minor and E♭ minor scales also have characteristics similar to the above group. The only difference is, that in B♭ minor, the three-finger groups of 2-3-4 and 4-3-2, though still mirroring each other, are not on all-black keys, and in E♭ minor, the two-finger groups of 2-3 and 3-2, though still mirroring each other, are not on all-black keys.

B♭ harmonic minor:

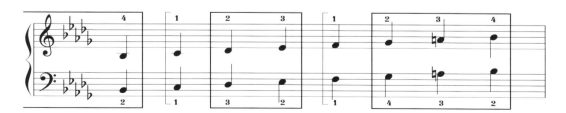

The harmonic C minor alternative fingerings of 2-3-4-1-2-3-1-2 in the RH and 4-3-2-1-3-2-1-4 in the LH also present similar reciprocal fingering in which thumbs are always together and on white keys, fingers 2-3 in one hand are always opposite fingers 3-2 in the other hand, and fingers 2-3-4 in one hand are always opposite fingers 4-3-2 in the other hand.

In using some of the alternative fingerings for scales, we can find ourselves playing the group of fingers 1-2-3 opposite the group of fingers 3-2-1, or the group of fingers 1-2-3-4 opposite 4-3-2-1, as well as the groups of fingers 1-2-3-4-5 and 5-4-3-2-1 opposite each other.

Following is the C major scale with an alternative fingering: two fingering groups of 1-2-3-4 are opposite two fingering groups of 4-3-2-1. This means that finger 1 in one hand is always played with finger 4 in the other hand and finger 2 in one hand is always played with finger 3 in the other hand.

The opening scale of the piano *Solo* entrance in Beethoven's *Concerto No. 3*, first movement, can be fingered this way, using two groups of the fingers 1-2-3-4 for each hand. This fingering will help achieve all the qualities this passage needs to convey, including the *sf* on the last note. As we do not necessarily have to start the group with its first finger, this fingering idea can present a number of fingering possibilities. The following example will show the most effective fingering possibilities that adhere to the above fingering ideas.

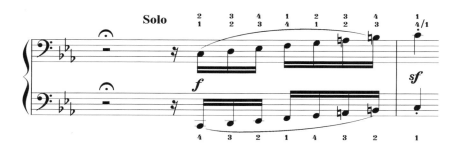

Let us check what happens with chromatic scales in this respect. Using the traditional fingering in parallel motion gives us fingers 3 of both hands always together and always on a black key. The thumbs are always together when they play on the white keys that are surrounded by two black keys. The groups of fingers 1-2 and 2-1 are opposite each other and play on the groups of two adjacent white keys that do not have a black key between them. Unlike C major and other similar scales, a chromatic scale in contrary motion starting on C will have no obvious correlation between the fingerings of the two hands; this makes it harder for the mind.

In order to get parallel fingering in both hands playing a chromatic scale in contrary motion, we would need to start on D or on G♯/A♭.

Let us check now what happens with arpeggios regarding reciprocal fingering. If we use finger 3 on the second arpeggio note in the LH root position for C major and other similar keys, we get the group of fingers 2-3 in one hand together with the group of fingers 3-2 in the other hand. We also get the thumbs played together in both hands, except for the bottom beginning in the LH, and the top end in the RH, where we play finger 5 of one hand together with finger 1 of the other hand. Starting the first inversion with fingers 1 and 5 in the respective hands will give us similar correlations as above, except that finger 4 replaces finger 3. That means that we get the group of fingers 2-4 in one hand together with the group of fingers 4-2 in the other hand. Starting the second inversion with fingers 1 and 5 in the respective hands, and using finger 3 on the third note in the RH, will give us the same correlations as in the root position – the group of fingers 2-3 in one hand together with the group of fingers 3-2 in the other hand, while thumbs are together except for the bottom and top ends.

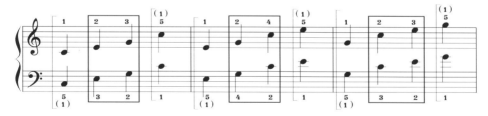

The keys of C♯ major/minor, A♭ major/minor, F♯ minor, and E♭ major, in their root position, give us the same correlations between the hands' fingerings as C major in the first inversion, except that the little fingers are not used here at all, so it is even simpler. The thumbs always play together, and the group of fingers 2-4 in one hand always plays together with the group of fingers 4-2 in the other hand; in other words, finger 2 in one hand is always played together with finger 4 in the other hand. Another correlation in this case is the fact that fingers 2 and 4 always play on black keys. Following is an example of C♯ minor.

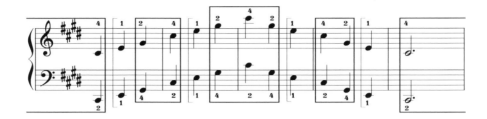

In Chopin's *Polonaise Op. 53 in A♭ major* we find four instances of this parallel B♭ minor melodic scale for both hands together, starting on the note A and ending on the note B♭. This passage spans three octaves the first time it appears and four octaves the other three times it appears. Using the idea of the connection between the fingerings of the two hands, as we saw above, makes a lot of sense, and makes it easy for the mind to execute.

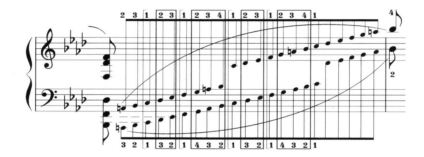

However, the power this passage needs to convey, being written twice in *forte* and two other times in *fortissimo*, may call for another fingering, perhaps more mentally demanding, but also more helpful for the desired execution of the passage. I suggest the following fingering for the LH in this passage: 3-2-1-4-3-2-1-3-2. Crossing in the LH from C to D♭ with fingers 1-4, and from G to A with fingers 1-3, is easier than crossing from F to G with fingers 1-4. This alternative fingering also gives a stronger ending to the passage with the LH fingers 1-3-2 instead of 4-3-2.

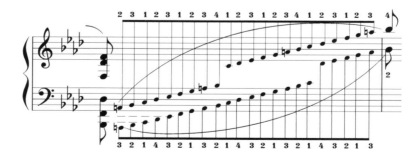

Can we find any connection between the fingerings of the two hands after we have changed the LH fingering to this alternative one? Yes, fingers 3 in both hands will play together, except for the very beginning of the passage, where fingers 2-3 in the RH is a stronger choice than fingers 3-4 which we otherwise use in this passage.

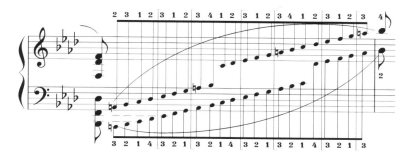

Of course, we can change around the RH fingering too, and get the following fingering which is both strong and mentally comfortable with regard to its correlation between the two hands.

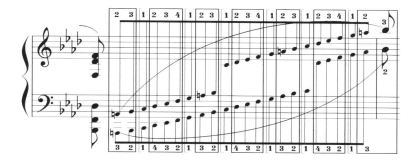

The *Secondo* part of the duet *Norwegian Dance No. 2* by Grieg has a parallel passage of sixteenth notes for both hands in the first two measures of the *Allegro* section. At first glance the following fingering may seem satisfactory.

Considering the fast tempo, the dynamic marking of *forte*, the accents, and the overall character, we may want to choose a fingering that is stronger. Following is my fingering suggestion for this passage.

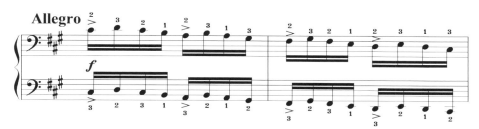

This fingering, which uses our strongest fingers, enables us to play with more power and articulation, but it may seem a little more taxing for the brain. Well, not really, if we can find the relationship between the fingerings of the two hands:

1.   The thumbs of both hands always play together.

2.   The group of fingers 2-3 in one hand always plays together with the group of fingers 3-2 in the other hand; in other words, finger 2 in one hand is always together with finger 3 in the other hand.

In addition, it is noteworthy that even though the note patterns consist of four sixteenth notes, and there are four such patterns in the sequence, the fingering patterns consist of eight sixteenth notes, and there are only two such patterns in the sequence.

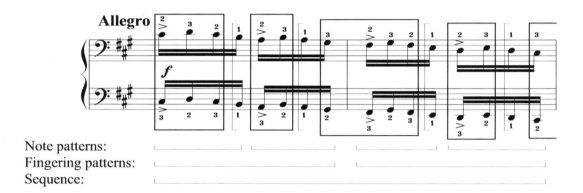

The last example here is the parallel passages in measures 5-6 of Chopin's *Revolutionary Étude Op. 10, No. 12*. The note patterns consist of eight sixteenth notes, and there are three (and three quarters) such patterns in the sequence, while the fingering patterns consist of only four sixteenth notes, and there are seven (and a half) such patterns in the sequence. Every note pattern consists of two fingering patterns. Is there a correlation between the fingerings of the two hands? Yes, there is, and an interesting one. Fingers 2 of both hands always play together and always fall on the accent. The group of fingers 1-4-3 in the RH is always opposite the group of fingers 4-3-1 in the LH.

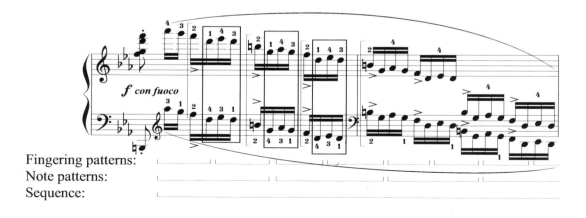

Redistribution of notes between the hands

Though some people may call it "cheating", this is a great tool used by all virtuosos of all times. It can simplify situations that may be unnecessarily complicated, result in better executions, and help keep the hands free from injury. After all, we are blessed with 10 fingers, and it wouldn't make sense not to take advantage of it. Speaking of "cheating", if Mozart could use his nose for playing the piano, we can certainly use all 10 fingers for playing the piano.

Redistribution, which can also be referred to as rewriting, means taking a note or a group of notes, vertically and/or horizontally, from the hand for which the notes seem to be written in the music, and playing it with the other hand.

I say "seems to be written in the music" because even though we have various rules and indications to point to the specific hand meant to be used, there are cases where the written score fails to make it clear. At any rate, I believe that the focus should be on the composer's intention of the end result, rather than on the composer's intention of how to get there, if there was one to begin with.

Bach's *Fugues* and other polyphonic music have this constant challenge of distributing and redistributing the middle voices between the two hands. The distribution suggestions of the middle voices vary among different editions, different teachers, different approaches, and of course one's own ideas.

The middle section of *Prelude No. 2* by Gershwin (*Largamente con moto*) even offers the choice of completely reversing the hands for the entire section or for any part of it. The melody here is in the bass line while the accompaniment is in the voices above. The idea behind the choice of reversing the hands is the notion that melody would be better executed with the RH. Personally, I do not take this choice here, and I play the melody in the LH. I also believe that both our hands should have equal ability. The next example shows the score as published, except that it bears my own fingering.

I would also point out that some people may like to redistribute between the two hands the notes written for the LH in the opening measures of this *Prelude No. 2*. Again, I personally do not take advantage of this tool here, as I would like the *legato* to be of a rocking type due to its *Blues* nature. Playing it as written in the LH gives me the sound and tilt that I want. My own personal fingering appears below the notes while another fingering possibility, requiring less of a stretch, appears above the notes.

The piano repertoire presents endless examples of redistribution possibilities. Following are some useful examples of redistribution.

Gershwin, *Prelude No. 2*, measure 10, take with the RH the LH notes B and B♯ (the longer bracket in the following example), or just the B♯ (the shorter bracket). Already at the beginning of the book we discussed how the assignment of notes to each hand is commonly indicated in the score: stems appearing up or down, actual LH and RH markings, and fingering written above or below the notes. In addition, brackets alone are also used to indicate playing specific notes with the other hand, as shown in the next example. Sometimes we may also find incomplete vertical brackets looking like a long letter L for taking a LH note in the RH, or an upside down long letter L for taking a RH note in the LH.

Measure 14 in the same *Prelude*, take with the RH the LH note B♯.

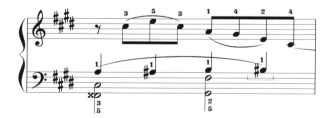

The accompaniment in the opening measures of *Consolation No. 3* by Liszt, which includes a bass note followed by a harmonic figuration, is written for the LH alone, so the RH will be free to enter with the melody. When the RH does enter with the melody and both hands play together we have no choice but to do as written. However, even though it is possible to play also the opening measures as written with the LH alone, since there is no RH melody to cover up little LH faults, this beginning is very exposed, and thus many pianists choose to rewrite it for both hands instead of just the LH. Now the question is which hand plays what. Either way can work, but if we do the harmonic figuration in the RH, we would have to switch to the LH in the middle of the third measure in order to free the RH for the melody notes. A smoother way is playing the bass note with the RH crossing over the LH, which plays the harmonic figuration, as follows.

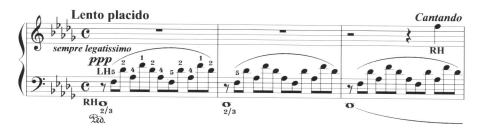

Liebesträume No. 3 by Liszt offers many redistributing opportunities. I shall suggest here three of them:

    1.   At the beginning of measure 25 – the *Cadenza* style measure, I suggest taking with the LH the bottom notes of the first 2 thirds in the RH, which are F♭ and E♭, thus playing in the LH three times F♭-E♭.

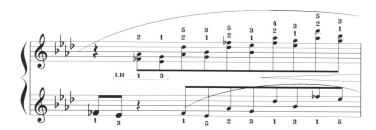

    2.   In measure 37, I suggest taking with the RH the first four notes of the descending zigzag arpeggio type in the LH.

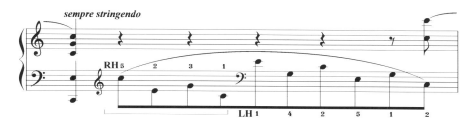

    3.   In measure 60, I suggest taking with the LH the first two bottom notes of the RH, D and E♭, and then just the E♭ one octave higher and two octaves higher.

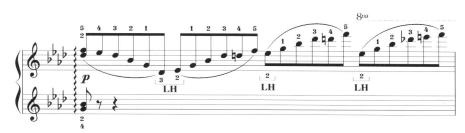

The Scarlatti D major *Sonata K. 29* (*L. 461* and *P. 85*) offers many redistributing opportunities. As a matter of fact, different editions suggest different and even contradicting note-distributions, let alone occasional differing text. I shall make suggestions regarding three places in the piece:

1. Measures 10-12. In measure 12, I switch the hands and the RH plays both the last three notes of measure 11, and the first note of measure 12.

2. Measure 33:

3. The first eight measures in the second half of the piece:

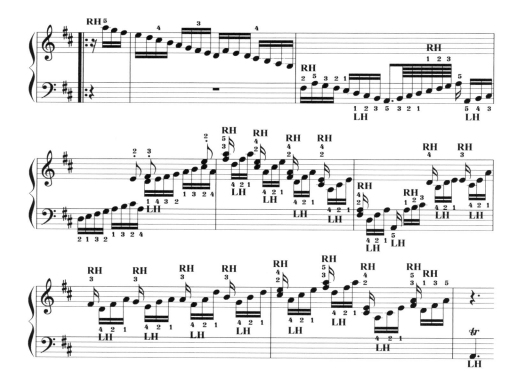

Let us look at Chopin, *Étude in C minor Op. 10, No. 12*, measure 9. There are many similar cases in the repertoire where the LH accompaniment starts alone, and the melody joins in a little later. Obviously, we should be able to play the LH as written, and by all means practice it as written. As a matter of fact, two measures later when the RH plays the melody, we do it anyway, as we do not have any other choice. However, when the LH is all alone and completely exposed, I suggest sharing the load with the RH as shown in the next example. This redistribution will also enhance the little dynamic swell marked in the music.

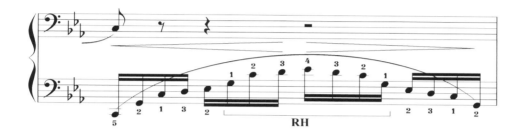

One of the classic examples for redistribution possibilities is the Scriabin *Etude Op. 8, No. 12*, which by the way is written under the rhythmical influence of the motif from the previous example – Chopin *Étude Op. 10, No. 12*. Like in the previous example, the LH is exposed with the accompaniment alone before the melody comes in. When the melody comes in there is no relief, as the LH has to make even bigger leaps in quite a lively tempo. The notes to which the LH has to jump are already within the range of the RH, some of them were actually just played by the RH, which is right there in the position to play them again instead of the LH having to leap to them. The following example shows the first four measures.

Beethoven's *Appassionata* has some interesting redistribution possibilities. Measures 44-46 of the first movement have in each one of them a RH trill which starts with a grace note. My redistribution suggestion here is to play the preceding grace note (F♭) in both measures 45 and 46 with the LH. Doing so helps with security and uniformity of execution: it avoids unnecessary leaps in the RH which are, otherwise, required when playing these trills, including their preceding and succeeding grace notes, with the RH alone; it also gives us uniformity in executing the trills which we won't otherwise have should we choose to play the second trill with the LH, as often suggested in various editions.

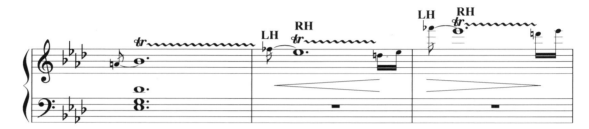

The second movement of the *Appassionata* also presents interesting redistribution possibilities in the third *Variation*. In the second ending of the second part of the second *Variation* there are seven thirty-second notes that actually start the third *Variation*. I suggest playing these seven notes with the RH, as indicated by the bracket shown in the following example.

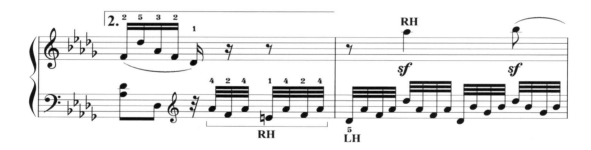

Three more spots in this *Variation* can benefit from redistribution: In measure 4 of the *Variation* I suggest playing with the RH the last three thirty-second notes written for the LH.

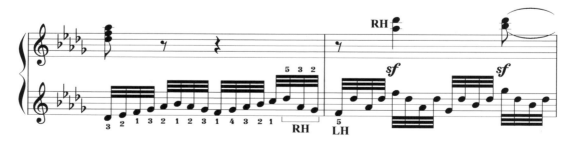

In measure 16 I suggest playing with the RH the last two thirty-second notes written for the LH, or even the last 11 thirty-second notes written for the LH, as shown in the next two examples.

The third spot is measure 24. I often take the change of hands from the second note in a group; if possible, I take it to the first note in the next group, as this also helps to shape the phrase.

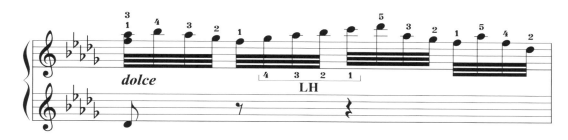

The last example here is *Erlkönig*, which was already discussed in "Repeated notes". Some people play it rewritten as follows.

Toccata style

Often we need to repeat the same note, alternating between the hands back and forth. This repetition can also be between a single note in one hand, and a chord or any harmonic interval, including the repeated note, in the other hand. It can also be between two chords, or between any two harmonic intervals, or between a chord and any harmonic interval.

The third movement of Gershwin, *Concerto in F* has a variety of such examples. Measures 51-54 of the first *Solo* show a single note repetition in the *Toccata* style.

In this *Toccata* style one hand should be distal on the keys (closer to the fall board) with a high wrist, while the other hand is proximal on the keys (closer to your body) with a low wrist. Wherever possible, it is best to try and avoid using the thumb, which, due to its shortness, may cause a "traffic jam" or a "collision" between the hands, as well as an unpleasant and unhealthy twist of the hand. In such cases of avoiding the thumbs, they can hang loose. The thumb of the hand with the low wrist hangs outside the keyboard line, almost like at the time in history when the thumb was not used at all for playing a keyboard instrument.

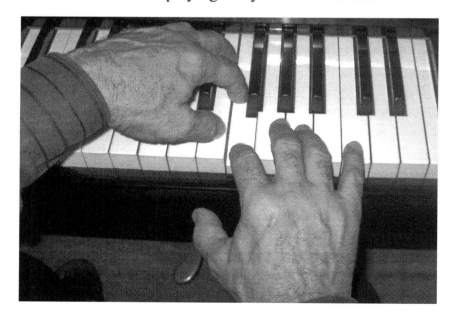

When not used, the thumbs can also be tucked under the palms, or support the playing fingers by touching them from behind. In the beginning measures of the third *Solo* we must use the RH thumb, but we have the choice of not using the LH thumb. Therefore I recommend the following fingering.

In the opening measures of the first *Solo* we also have a case where one hand uses the thumb and the other hand does not use the thumb.

The hand that is using the thumb would normally be playing underneath the hand that is not using the thumb.

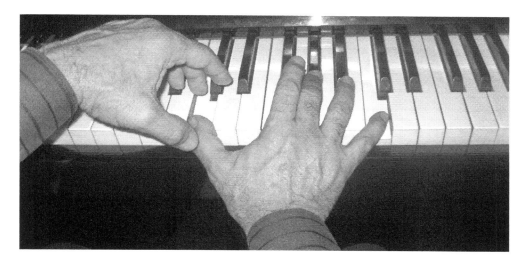

The same ideas also apply when there is no mutual note being repeated in both hands, in which case the sound texture is more like a trill or a *tremolo*.

Crossing hands and interlocking

As in *Toccata* style, when crossing hands it is best to try and avoid using the thumbs, particularly in the crossing hand. In this case, the thumb of the hand which is crossing above the other hand hangs loose outside the keyboard line.

Gershwin's *Rhapsody in Blue* has quite a variety of hand crossings and *Toccata* style playing. Measures 13-16 in the "locomotive-motive" section (*Agitato e misterioso*) have both *Toccata style* note-repetition and hand crossings.

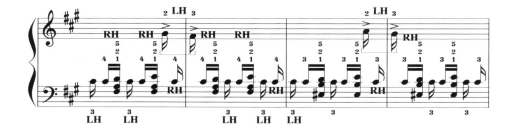

Avoiding the thumb is especially important when the RH plays further to the left on the keyboard, and the LH plays further to the right on the keyboard.

Two such examples are to be found at the very end of the following two pieces by Debussy:

1. The last chord of *Jardins sous la pluie* (*Gardens in the rain*) has the LH crossing over the RH to play the highest E of the piano.

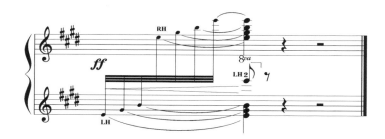

2.   The last note of *L'isle Joyeuse* (*The Island of Pleasure*) has the RH crossing over the LH to play the lowest A of the piano. In this case, where the dynamic marking is *triple forte* and the note is marked with a strong accent, I would suggest that it be played with two fingers together, 2 and 3.

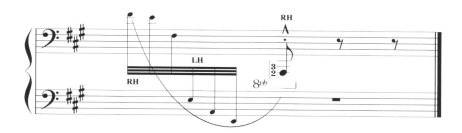

Unless the thumb is needed, the above can also be applied when the crossing hand has to play two or more notes together.

Two such examples are to be found in *Sonatine* by Ravel:
1.   In the first movement, two measures before the first ending, the LH crosses over the RH and plays two notes together.

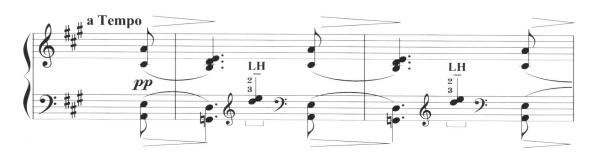

2.   The very last chord of the piece has the LH crossing over the RH and playing two notes together.

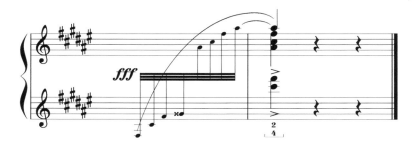

Of course there are endless examples in the repertoire, but the following example is interesting, as it enables one to reverse the hands while still keeping the same principle of not using the thumb (if possible) when crossing hands. The example is, once again, the *D major Sonata, K. 29* by Scarlatti, measure four in the second half of the piece. Two fingering possibilities are shown: first, the RH crossing over the LH, playing two notes together and fingered without the thumb.

Now, for the same music, the hands are reversed and the example shows the LH crossing over the RH, playing two notes together and fingered without the thumb.

The same "rule of thumb", or rather rule of no-thumb (when possible), also applies to interlocking passages and chord trills or to any sort of passages where one hand plays over the other. The hand which plays on more black keys will usually be the one playing or crossing above while, of course, also playing inward on the keys (distal), and with a high wrist. The hand which plays on more white keys will usually be the one playing or crossing underneath while, of course, also playing outward on the keys (proximal), and with a low wrist.

The following example is from the unique passages in the *Chinese Variation* of Gershwin's *I Got Rhythm Variations*, where the hands play together in intervals of minor seconds. In measures 34-37 of the *Chinese Variation* (*Allegretto giocoso*) the LH, which has a key signature of six sharps and plays only on the black keys, should be above the RH, which has a key signature of just one sharp and plays only on the white keys.

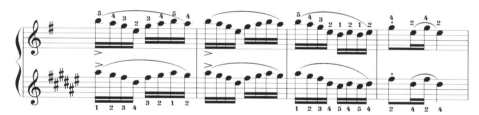

When we have interlocking passages that move up and/or down in *Toccata* style, it is best not to repeat the same finger for all the notes in one hand, but to set the hands to arpeggio or scale fingering according to the text requirements. Blocking groups of notes into hand positions can improve speed and security of execution.

The following passage is from measure 17 of the *Hungarian Rhapsody No. 11* by Liszt. The LH notes form an ascending major arpeggio starting on the note G♯. Using fingering that covers the blocked four-note chord is preferred to using the same finger for each of the different arpeggio notes. If we avoid the thumb, we get the fingering of 5-3-2 for the LH.

The next example shows my suggested fingering for the *Cadenza* part of measure 67 in the *Rigoletto Concert Paraphrase* by Liszt. This particular case also shows that the fingering groups and blocks do not necessarily have to correspond to the rhythmical groups or to the melodic groups of notes.

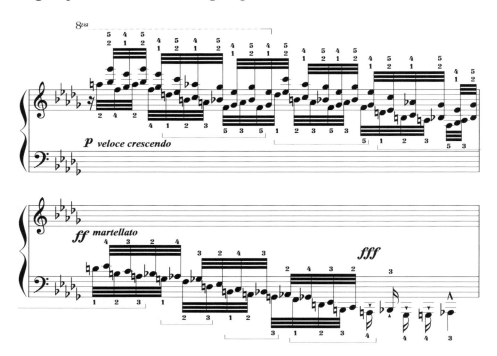

The last example here is also from the *Chinese Variation* of Gershwin's *I Got Rhythm Variations*. In this instance, all the note groupings do correspond with the blocked fingerings. Measures 48-49 of the *Chinese Variation* (*Allegretto giocoso*):

Glissandos

Glissandos are done mostly with the nails. When it is not possible to use the nail, we use the cushion of the finger.

Ascending in the RH and descending in the LH is mostly done with an open hand turned over so the palm is facing up (supination), using the nails of fingers 3 and 4 together as if the fingers are glued to each other. Some people use fingers 2, 3, and 4 together, especially for a more vigorous *glissando*. Fingers 2 and 3 together are also good, and either finger is good too for a gentler *glissando*. When using more than one finger for this technique of *glissando*, one may have to adjust the angle of the hand in relation to the fall board due to the different lengths of the fingers. The RH will point to the left, and the LH will point to the right. The hand will be diagonal to the keyboard surface, with or without the support of the thumb.

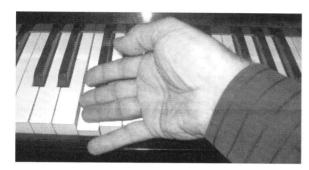 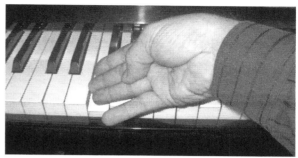

Descending in the RH and Ascending in the LH is mostly done using the nail of the thumb. The hand stays in a fairly normal playing position while some tilting towards the thumb may help. As we move towards the center of the keyboard the hand starts pointing outwards – wrist pointing inward.

Here too we can add the support of the other fingers. We need to hold the other fingers against the thumb, making the shape of a bird's beak, (next photo on the left). With the hand shaped like a bird's beak we do the same *glissando* using the nail of the thumb as described above (next photo on the right).

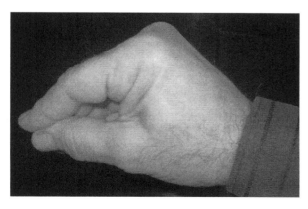 

It is possible to use the thumb nail also for the RH ascending and the LH descending, though I prefer using the nails of fingers 2, 3, and 4 in the various combinations, as mentioned above. It is also possible to use the nails of fingers 2, 3, and 4 in the various combinations for the RH descending and LH ascending, but I find it uncomfortable and unhealthy for the hands, and therefore unnecessary. The above glissando techniques that I prefer also work well when a fast change of direction is required. One doesn't need to completely turn the hand in the opposite direction; a simple forearm rotation will take care of a very smooth and injury-free transition.

The above *glissando* techniques are as good for the white keys as they are for the black keys; they can produce *forte* or *piano* or any other dynamics. However, there is another technique for *glissandos* which can produce a smoother *legato* sound, is easier than the previous one to execute on the black keys, and is particularly beautiful in *piano* and *pianissimo*. Fingers 2, 3, 4, and 5 are held over-curved and together as if creating one long nail, with or without the support of the thumb.

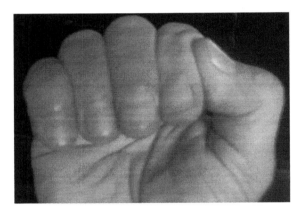

We hold the hand in a normal playing position, palms facing down (pronation), while the nails touch the keyboard, almost lying flat on it, but somewhat diagonally. The hand can travel in this position to the right and to the left, thus creating this *glissando*. A slight turn of the hand in the direction of the movement and/or a slight down tilt in the opposite direction of the movement can help this *glissando*. The next photo on the left shows the hand position without the support of the thumb and the photo on the right shows the hand position with the support of the thumb.

 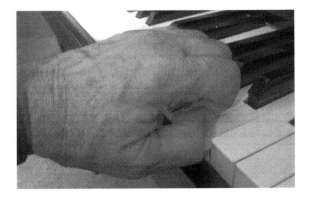

The difference between this *glissando* technique and the previous ones is that, in the previous ones, one key had to be let go when the next key was depressed, whereas in this technique, the previous key stays down when three more nails go over it, thus creating quite an overlapping *legato*. It is best to start practicing any glissando without actual sound except for the sound of the nails on the keys.

Glissandos can be done in harmonic intervals and even in some chords with one hand. Not all chords are possible or practical, and some are better executed in one direction than in the other, if at all.

The important idea of such *glissandos* is that the hand stays more or less in a normal playing position and does not turn over with palms up like in the first *glissando* technique discussed above. The fingers must be very curved, but not over-curved like in the last single-note *glissando* technique. In small intervals of up to a fifth, the hand does need to turn in the direction of the movement. The fingers to use are 2 and 3, 2 and 4, 2 and 5, or 3 and 5.

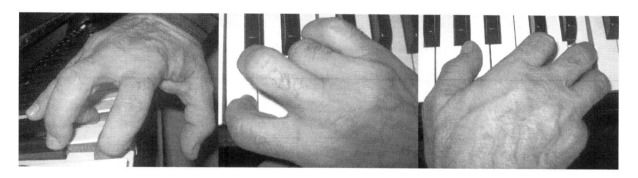

In intervals larger than a fifth, the hand does not turn and only one nail is involved; the other finger is now flat and has to slide on the finger cushion underneath the nail. "Sweaty" or "oily" keyboards do help here. Some pianists use a quick tongue lick of the finger cushion before starting a *glissando* of this kind. This is usually done with fingers 1 and 5. RH ascending and LH descending *glissandos* will be done with the nail of the little finger and the thumb cushion, as shown in the next photo on the left. RH descending and LH ascending *glissandos* will be done with the thumb nail and the little finger's cushion, as shown in the photo on the right.

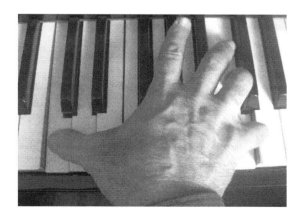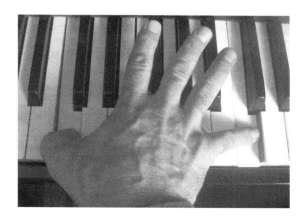

The intervals of a sixth and a seventh can also be done with fingers 1 and 4 in the same manner. Using fingers 1 and 3 is also possible, mainly for a *glissando* in double sixths, but due to the stretch it poses, perhaps it is less desirable.

Finger pedaling

Finger pedaling, also referred to as the prolonged touch or as over-holding, is created by holding fingers down on played keys while continuing to play other keys. It is a wonderful traditional tool, already used on the harpsichord and on other pre-piano keyboard instruments. Finger pedaling may be spelled out in the music, or it may be the player's choice of articulation.

In the Baroque and early Classical periods of music, finger pedaling was a natural part of the keyboard player's technique and a common performance practice. This style of playing derived mainly from keyboard instruments preceding the piano. These instruments had no damper pedal to help with sustaining notes, and except for the organ, they had a weak sound with a fast decay.

A classic example of finger pedaling written out in the notation is *Prelude No. 1* in *Book I* of *WTC* by Bach. The two bottom voices are constantly held through half of the measure. The following example shows the first four measures of the *Prelude*.

Another example is Mozart *Sonata in D major K. 311*, second movement, measures 8-11, where the bass notes are held as quarter notes while the other accompaniment notes are played.

Another similar example is Beethoven *Sonata in F major Op. 10, No. 2*, first movement, measures 30-35. Here too the bass notes are held as quarter notes while the other accompaniment notes are played.

It is quite interesting to note how Anna Magdalena Bach copied the *Rondeau* (*Les Bergerie*s) by Couperin into her *Little Notebook* (*Clavierbüchlein*). Couperin's original music had finger pedaling spelled out for the LH as we can see in the opening measures.

A.M.B. must have taken finger pedaling for granted, for she notated the same opening measures as follows:

The tool of finger pedaling can be very helpful when playing without using the sustain pedal or when pedaling needs to be cleared while some extra resonance and overtones are still desired. It can also be very effective when we wish to bring out some extra hidden voices/melodies in the music. Alberti bass and similar accompaniments can benefit from it, with or without the use of the sustain pedal. One interpretation of the short slurs often appearing over harmonic groups of four sixteenth notes like Alberti bass and other similar passages in the Classical period, is finger pedaling. Of course, one has to be careful not to lose clarity by keeping the fingers down on played keys indefinitely and for no reason, which would be a rather sloppy sort of piano playing. Finger pedaling like everything else should be done only intentionally when so desired. Consideration should be given to the period of the music and its performance practice; consideration should also be given to present-time performance practices and acceptable styles of playing.

In the second movement of the Haydn D major *Concerto* I would use finger pedaling in both endings of the first *Solo* and the second *Solo*. This would help enhance the lines already played by the orchestra as well as give the *Solo* part more presence. Holding the eighth notes with finger pedaling brings out these extra hidden voices. Measure 30:

Measure 44:

Chopin's *Sonata No. 3, Op. 58 in B minor*, which already has many spots of written-out finger pedaling, can benefit from the use of some additional finger pedaling in the second theme of the first movement. When eighth notes in the melody move in steps against the harmonic triplets in the accompaniment, the sustain pedal cannot stay down. Clearing the pedal will create a void, and changing it on every eighth note in the melody may make it restless-sounding and not flowing continuously. An elegant solution would be finger pedaling as shown in the next example by the added voices and slurs on the last three notes of the LH. Measure 41:

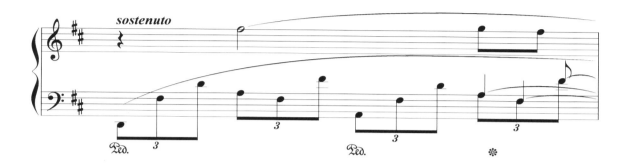

A similar problem appears in measures 72-75 of Chopin's *Ballade No. 1 in G minor.* Following is my suggested solution using finger pedaling in the LH. Not every hand can reach the interval of a tenth, therefore the whole note appearing along with every third quarter in the measure is optional.

Chopin uses a lot of spelled-out finger pedaling in this *Ballade.* However, an opportunity for using additional finger pedaling in the best tradition of the Romantic period's grand playing style would be the ascending RH passage in measures 130-133. Holding each of the bottom notes for a quarter instead of the written eighth, and playing them as *legato* as possible will bring out this exotic-sounding octatonic scale, also known in jazz as the diminished scale, which is made of ascending notes in alternating intervals of a whole step and a half step. This is shown written out in the following music example.

Clusters

The most commonly used *avant-garde* piano technique is clusters. Clusters are marked in the score in various ways, and usually with an added explanation. They are often marked as shown in the next example, my own *Rhapsody in Blue and White*, measure 141, LH.

cluster (black & white keys)

For small clusters we can use straight and bunched fingers. For *forte* small clusters we can use the open palm of a flat hand pointing straight forward. For stronger small clusters we can use the back cushion of the palm with fingers stretched forward on white keys or very curved, almost like a fist, on black keys. For very small and very powerful clusters, played on white or on black keys, we can use the fist sideways or the elbow with an open hand or a fist. For clusters consisting of black and white keys, we can lay straight and bunched fingers on the black keys while the back cushion of the palm is laid on the white keys. For large-span clusters we may use the entire palm and fingers pointing sideways in either direction, abducted or adducted. Towards the low range of the keyboard, the hands will point to the left, and towards the high range of the keyboard, the hands will point to the right. For larger-span clusters we can use the entire forearm and palm, sideways of course, while the right elbow points to the right of the keyboard and the left elbow points to the left of the keyboard. Following are photos of several cluster execution possibilities.

  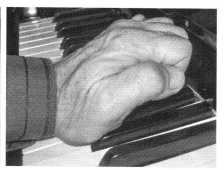

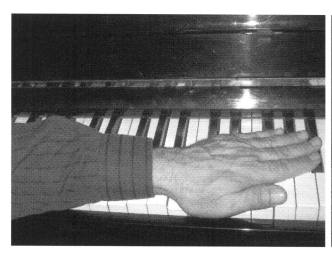  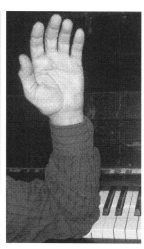

General advice about technique

Whenever the thumb plays on a black key you might want to somewhat extend it beyond its normal position, as shown in the next photo, so it doesn't slip off.

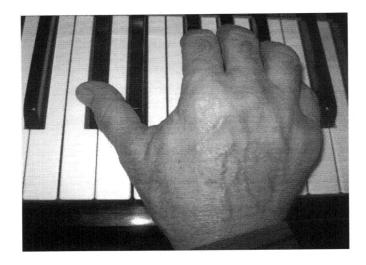

Other fingers on black keys are often more secure when played less curved and somewhat diagonally, especially as we get closer to the extreme ends of the keyboard, as shown in the next two photos.

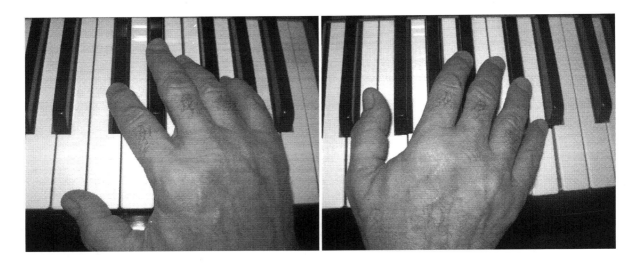

Any time we have prolonged similar movements it would be good to try and change the sets of muscles involved in the movements as we go along, in order to prevent excess tension build-up and repetitive strain injury. Changing the sets of muscles will occur when we change fingerings, and when we change the technical approach and hand angles. Momentary tension does not pose danger to hands' health as long as it is released almost immediately.

Doubles

Trills in double thirds

The most straightforward fingering for trills in double thirds is 1\3-2\4 in the RH and its mirror 3\1-4\2 in the LH. However, some alternatives may prove better at times. First, a simple variation, as we have seen before, skip a finger and use finger 5 instead of finger 4, thus trilling with RH fingers 1\3-2\5 and its mirror LH 3\1-5\2. Normally, a particular fingering discussed for the RH needs to be mirrored by the LH playing the same in contrary motion. A variation on the variation would be, instead of finger 3 use finger 4, thus trilling with 1\4-2\5. Other useful alternatives are 2\4-1\5, 2\3-1\4, and 2\3-1\5. In most cases where the bottom note of the lower pair of notes in the RH trill is a black key (top note of the higher pair of notes in the LH), it is advisable to avoid using the thumb on it.

Here are a number of feasible possibilities for the RH in the first measure of the *Thirds Étude Op. 25, No. 6* by Chopin.

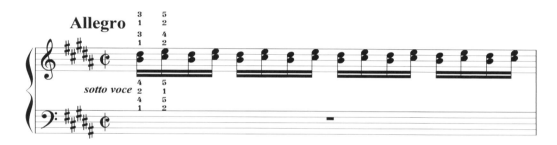

I did not give the possibilities of using 2\3-1\4 and 2\3-1\5 in the above example because fingers 2\3 on this specific interval of a major third B\D♯ would cause an unpleasant and unhealthy stretch. However, in Mendelssohn's *Rondo Capriccioso* I would not hesitate to use the fingering of 2\3-1\4 and 2\3-1\5 because in this case fingers 2\3 fall on a minor third, which is a friendlier interval for this type of fingering. This is especially true when the bottom note of the minor third in the RH is a black key. Of course using fingers 2\4-1\5 here is as good. Of the three fingering possibilities shown in measures 18-20 of the *Presto*, I personally prefer to use fingers 2\3-1\5.

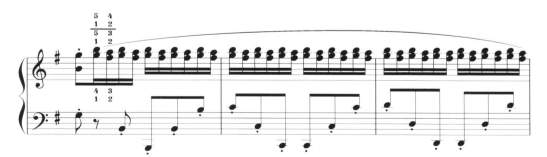

In the first movement of Beethoven's *Concerto No. 4* there are RH passages of trills in double thirds while the LH plays chromatic scales, and then joins in also with a trill. These trills appear twice in different keys, once before the *Tutti* leading to the development section, and the second time in the recapitulation before the *Tutti* leading to the *Cadenza*. Both times these trills in double thirds are four measures long, therefore, I suggest changing the fingering somewhere around halfway. Since the lower pair of notes is a minor third with a black key as the bottom note, we can use fingers 2\3 or 2\4 on this pair, just like in the Mendelssohn example above. Since the third finger plays on the D♯ leading into the trill (not shown in the music example), I suggest starting with fingers 2\4-1\5, immediately changing to 2\3-1\5, and then, a little later on, changing back to 2\4-1\5, as shown in the next example, measures 166-169.

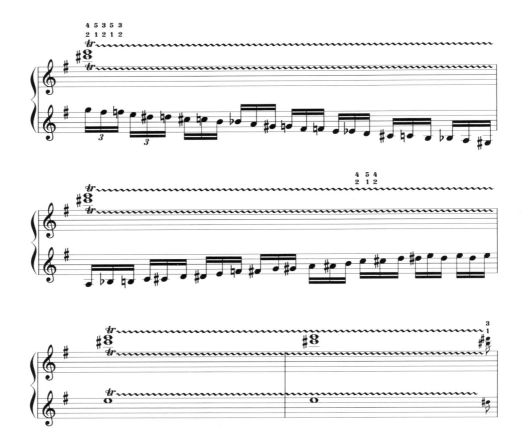

Trills in double fourths

As with double thirds, we first consider the obvious RH fingering 1\4-2\5, then the useful alternative 2\4-1\5. This alternative is especially valid when the lower pair of notes includes one or two black keys. For the LH, simply mirror the RH fingering. The third movement of Beethoven's *Concerto No. 4* has such a trill for the

RH in measures 5-8 after the *Cadenza*. Using fingers 2\4-1\5 would be very useful here. The number of times the fingerings repeat on trilled notes in the example does not suggest the density of the trill.

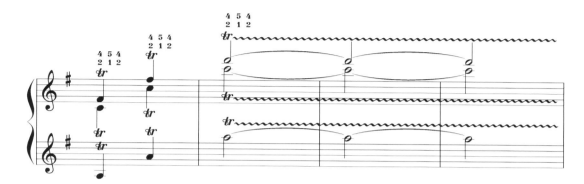

In some cases it is also possible to *tremolo* between the two bottom notes and the two top notes of the trill. If done very fast and while something else is going on in the music, it is quite hard to tell the difference. In this example, the LH also has trills going on at the same time as the trills of fourths in the RH. Doing a *tremolo* in the RH instead of a regular double trill is quite a good idea here.

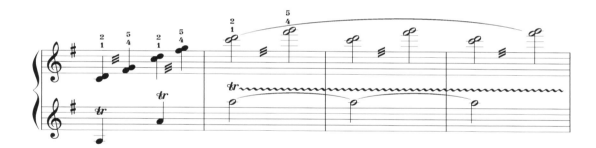

There are other possibilities for executing this type of trill, as will be discussed next.

Trills in Chords

Even theoretically it is not possible to trill three voices with six different notes in one hand. We would need six fingers for it but we have only five. What we can do is trill chords using the two hands alternately as in *Toccata* style, each hand playing a different chord. The technique is like when crossing hands and interlocking, one hand above and in front of the other. The same Beethoven's *Concerto No. 4* trill appearing five measures after the end of the third movement *Cadenza*, can also be played this way. The LH plays the chord A\C\F♯ and alternates with the RH that plays the chord B\D\G. The LH fingering can be 5\3\1, and the RH fingering can be

2\3\5. If this trill remained in a single register I would consider the fingering 5\4\2 for the LH, but the quick jump into the trill and the immediately-following two consecutive jumps of one octave, all in *forte*, are safer with the fingering 5\3\1. The LH has one black key and therefore plays above the RH which has only white keys.

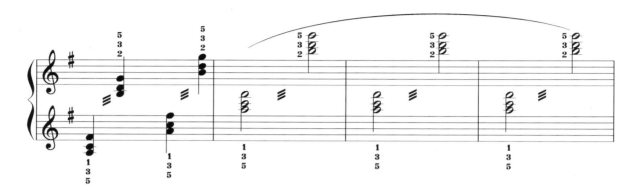

In the Grieg *Concerto,* 17-18 measures from the end of the first movement, we find a trill in chords which is written out in the *Toccata* style and is meant to be played by alternating the two hands. There are three notes in the LH chord and only two notes in the RH which change from F\C to E\C. Avoiding the thumbs here may cause a slight unpleasant stretch. Therefore, in this case I would use the thumb in both hands; the LH will be on top of the RH.

There is also the possibility of executing this *trill* in a non-*Toccata* style with the following redistribution of notes between the hands. This can be a good option, considering the soft dynamics called for.

In *Scarbo* from *Gaspard de la Nuit*, Ravel gives us a chord trill with a three-note chord in the LH and a five-note chord in the RH. Considering the *fortissimo* this trill has to reach, there is only one practical way of executing it, which is the way it is written. Therefore, there is only one possible fingering. Measures 23-29:

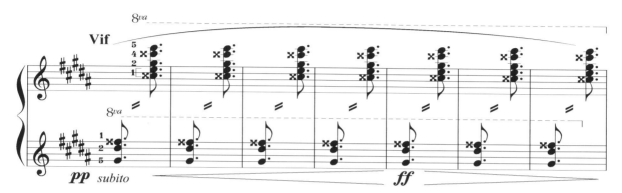

Semi-double trills

I may have made up a term here, referring to trilling in one hand between two or even three notes on one side of the trill, and a single note or two notes on the other side. Basically, there are two execution possibilities, one is as written and the other is as a *tremolo*. When the other hand is free, there could be a third way of execution, which is the *Toccata* style discussed earlier.

In the first movement of the Grieg *Concerto* we have such trills at the end of the exposition and at the end of the recapitulation. These would probably be done best as written, which is trilling between D\F\B at the bottom and C at the top. They can also be done as *tremolos*, especially when played fast. The advantage of playing a *tremolo* over the written trill is that we don't have to trill between fingers 4 and 5. The next two examples from the last *Solo* measure of the exposition show two ways of playing the *tremolo* in the RH. One way is playing the *tremolo* between the two bottom notes and the two top notes.

The other way is playing the *tremolo* between one note at the bottom, played with the thumb, and three notes at the top.

This type of semi-double trill also appears in the first movement of Chopin, *Concerto No. 1 in E minor*. It is interesting to note that it appears in the same two spots as in the Grieg *Concerto*, at the end of the exposition and at the end of the recapitulation. This trill is already written as a sort of *tremolo*, and is probably best played as written, which is trilling between A\B\F♯ at the bottom and G♯\B at the top. However, the *tremolo* form of the thumb playing on one side (this time playing simultaneously on two notes) against the other notes in the chord on the other side, can also be effective. This is shown in the next example, the last four measures of the *Solo* in the exposition.

At the end of *Concerto No. 1 in D minor* by Brahms, 10 and 11 measures from the end, and in his *Concerto No. 2 in B♭ major*, measure 173 of the first movement, there are semi-double trills similar to those in the Grieg *Concerto* mentioned above. They can be played as written, or in any of the *tremolo* forms suggested above.

In the first movement of the Brahms *D minor Concerto*, as well as at the end of the first movement of the *B♭ major Concerto*, we find RH *fortissimo* trills between a double octave and a single note above it. Some of these trills can be played with fingers 3 and 5 on top, if we have the hand span to play a double octave with fingers 1 and 3. Otherwise, we have to play the trills with fingers 4 and 5. In addition to playing these trills the way they are written, they can also be executed as *tremolos*.

Measures 20-21 of the first *Solo* in the first movement of the *D minor Concerto*:

These trills can also be executed as chord trills (double-octave trills in this particular case) in *Toccata* style with minor rewriting of the notes. This is quite effective, and is especially good for pianists who cannot play *fortissimo* double octaves with fingers 1 and 4 either.

Scales in double thirds

While scales in double thirds cannot always be played in perfect *legato*, one of the fingering concerns here is the ability to play as *legato* as possible. Obviously, *legato* fingering can be used for *staccato* or *non-legato* playing, but *staccato* fingering is not necessarily good for producing *legato* playing.

There are various good fingerings based on the traditional principle of using position groups of fingers, and crossing between them. The main two position groups are the full five-finger one 1\3-2\4-3\5 and the shorter one 1\3-2\4. Playing just the white keys enables us to change the order of the fingering groups as they appear in the scale, and use any of the six examples as shown here for each hand.

Examples for **C major RH** ascending: 1\3-2\4-3\5-1\3-2\4-1\3-2\4-1\3...
or   1\3-2\4-1\3-2\4-3\5-1\3-2\4-1\3...   or   1\3-2\4-1\3-2\4-1\3-2\4-3\5-1\3...
or   2\4-1\3-2\4-3\5-1\3-2\4-1\3-2\4...   or   2\4-1\3-2\4-1\3-2\4-3\5-1\3-2\4...
or   3\5-1\3-2\4-1\3-2\4-1\3-2\4-3\5...

Examples for **C major LH** ascending: 5\3-4\2-3\1-4\2-3\1-4\2-3\1-5\3...
or   3\1-4\2-3\1-5\3-4\2-3\1-4\2-3\1...   or   3\1-4\2-3\1-4\2-3\1-5\3-4\2-3\1...
or   3\1-5\3-4\2-3\1-4\2-3\1-4\2-3\1...   or   4\2-3\1-5\3-4\2-3\1-4\2-3\1-4\2...
or   4\2-3\1-4\2-3\1-5\3-4\2-3\1-4\2...

Both hands can return with the same fingering in reverse order. We can take advantage of these six possibilities for each hand and mix and match them when playing both hands together. We can achieve better *legato* sound and smoothness if we see to it that the crossings do not occur at the same time in both hands.

Using the RH ascending fingering 1\3-2\4-3\5-1\3-2\4-1\3-2\4-1\3

with the LH ascending fingering   5\3-4\2-3\1-4\2-3\1-4\2-3\1-5\3

will give us three crossings at the same time.

Using the RH ascending fingering of one octave 1\3-2\4-3\5-1\3-2\4-1\3-2\4-3\5

with the LH ascending fingering   4\2-3\1-4\2-3\1-5\3-4\2-3\1-4\2

will give us no crossings at the same time. If we do more than one octave, we have to change the fingering on the last pair of notes in the RH from 3\5 to 1\3, and that will give us only one crossing in both hands at the same time.

This luxury of choosing different fingerings becomes somewhat less possible as we get into scales with black keys. This happens because, in certain cases, we try to avoid using the thumb on black keys due to its shortness. Also, the little finger is not always comfortable and safe on the black keys; altogether some crossings between pairs of fingers playing thirds are less smooth when we play on the black keys.

For two octaves, we can also use the same full five-finger position group 1\3-2\4-3\5 repeatedly in both hands, and in either direction. This type of fingering does not repeat itself in every octave – something we will see more often as we go along. For the two octaves, it looks like this:

RH ascending 1\3-2\4-3\5-1\3-2\4-3\5-1\3-2\4-3\5-1\3-2\4-3\5-1\3-2\4-3\5;

LH ascending 5\3-4\2-3\1-5\3-4\2-3\1-5\3-4\2-3\1-5\3-4\2-3\1-5\3-4\2-3\1.

Both hands can return with the same fingering in reverse order. Obviously, if we play this fingering hands together, the crossings will occur in both hands at the same time, but there will be one less crossing than in any other fingering that repeats itself in every octave. The above fingering makes a nice exercise in any scale and mode.

Here is another suggested finger exercise for playing double thirds. Though the exercise is written in C major, it can and should be done in all keys, major, minor, and any other modes.

All the above double-thirds fingerings involve only two types of crossings between pairs of fingers:
1. Crossing between the two pairs of fingers 3\5 and 1\3.
2. Crossing between the two pairs of fingers 2\4 and 1\3.

Therefore, the following exercise for crossing pairs of fingers would prove very useful too. Even though it is possible, it is not meant to be played hands together. However if one does play hands together, mixing and matching of the fingerings can be done as well.

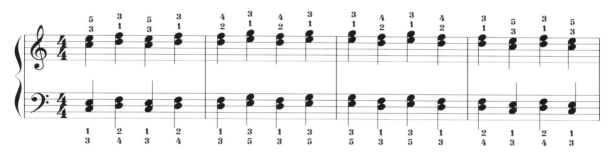

In general, fingering ideas which are based on larger single fingering groups and fewer finger crossings, will better serve speed and a lighter touch, while fingering which utilizes smaller single fingering groups can better serve clearer articulation and a heavier touch. Two additional fingering suggestions will broaden the possibilities and may also help improve some of these passages in various cases. These suggestions will involve "odd" pairs of fingers like 1\2 and 1\5, which are not one finger apart (skipping a finger):

1. At the beginning of a passage or a five-finger position group, ascending in the RH and descending in the LH, I would like to suggest using the fingering 1\2 going to 1\3. It is again like gaining an extra finger without using the tool of crossing fingers. If we use larger position groups, we will encounter fewer crossings in the course of a scale, a tactic that can enhance speed. This new extended position group of fingering is now 1\2-1\3-2\4-3\5. This works in reverse order too, so it can also be used when descending in the RH and ascending in the LH. Once again, the above fingering suggestion makes a nice exercise.

2.   At the end of a passage or a full five-finger position group, ascending in the RH and descending in the LH, I suggest using the fingering pair 1\5 instead of 3\5. This can also be effective at the beginning of a descending passage in the RH and an ascending one in the LH, as well as in a high change-of-direction point for a RH passage, and in a low one for a LH passage. We do use the same idea of going from fingers 2\4 to fingers 1\5 or from 1\5 to 2\4 as one of the fingering possibilities for a trill in double thirds, since double-thirds trilling between fingers 2\4 and 3\5 is not too common. We might, as well, take advantage of this idea and use it for scales in double thirds as described at the beginning of this paragraph.

The above extra fingering ideas can offer the following different fingerings for the C major RH ascending double-thirds scale in two or more octaves:
    1\2-1\3-2\4-3\5-1\3-2\4-3\5-1\2... or 1\3-2\4-3\5-1\2-1\3-2\4-3\5-1\3...
or 1\2-1\3-2\4-1\5-1\3-2\4-3\5-1\2... or 1\3-2\4-1\5-2\4-1\3-2\4-3\5-1\3...
    or, if we end just an octave above the notes we started:
    1\2-1\3-2\4-3\5-1\2-1\3-2\4-1\5, or 1\2-1\3-2\4-1\5-2\4-1\3-2\4-1\5,
or 1\3-2\4-1\5-2\4-1\3-2\4-1\5-2\4, or 1\3-2\4-3\5-1\3-2\4-1\5-2\4-1\5,
or 1\2-1\3-2\4-1\5-1\3-2\4-1\5-2\4. Return with the same fingering in reverse order. For the LH fingerings, just mirror the RH fingerings as we do in contrary motion.

The tool of starting and finishing scales in double thirds with fingers 1\2-1\3 at the bottom end of the RH and at the top end of the LH can be put to good use in the next two instances from Beethoven, *Concerto No. 4*, first movement. In measure 86 (measure 13 of the first *Solo* entrance) we first tend to accept this seemingly natural

RH fingering which can be found in one or two editions of the piece.

I suggest the RH fingering below, where finger 2 is on C, the top note of the third A\C. Starting the thirds with fingers 1\2 on the notes A\C, lets us play fingers 1\3 on the notes B\D and 2\4 on the notes C\E. This fingering enables a better crossing from fingers 2\4 on the notes C\E to fingers 1\3 on the notes D\F♯ than the above-suggested crossing from fingers 3\5 to fingers 1\3. It is always better if we do not use the same finger on both sides of the crossing. In the above example finger 3 has to travel from the key C to the key F♯. In the following example, where we play C\E with 2\4, finger 3 is free and with the hand's movement it is practically already above where it needs to be, which is F♯.

In measure 233 (measure 42 of the development *Solo* entrance) I suggest the following fingering, which, as mentioned before in "Same finger on different keys", makes for a much-safer jump from the last sixteenth note to the next quarter note.

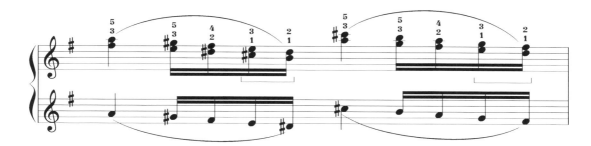

Following are a number of examples for the use of the thumb instead of finger 3 when played along with the little finger in scales in double thirds.

The first measure of Beethoven, *Sonata in C major Op. 2, No. 3*:

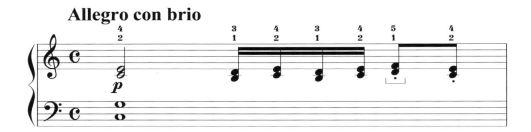

Mozart *Sonatas* offer many such opportunities for both hands. The next two examples are for the left hand in the third movement of the *C major Sonata K. 279*. I would use this fingering idea in measures 1-2, 5-6, and all similar places if possible.

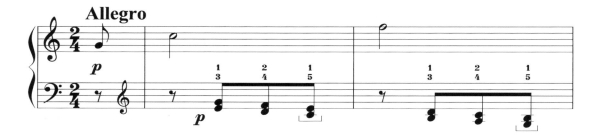

I would use this fingering idea in particular in measures 16-17.

The first movement of Beethoven's *Concerto No. 4* offers a few such opportunities for the right hand: the third sixteenth in the third beat of measure 88 (measure 15 of the first *Solo* entrance); the third sixteenth in the fourth beat of measure 234 (measure 43 of the development *Solo* entrance); the first sixteenth in the fourth beat of measure 110 (measure 18 of the second *Solo* entrance). The latter will also serve as our next music example. It is the end of the double-thirds trill which we do anyway with the fingering 2\4 and 1\5. We would not think of doing this double-thirds trill with fingers 2\4 and 3\5 which would be quite difficult for most people. There is no reason not to use the same fingering idea (which puts fingers 1\5 on the higher pair of notes E\G) also after the *nachschlag*. Incidentally, the last two pairs of notes in the RH of this example will also show the use of fingers

1\2-1\3 successively, though this time not in *legato*.

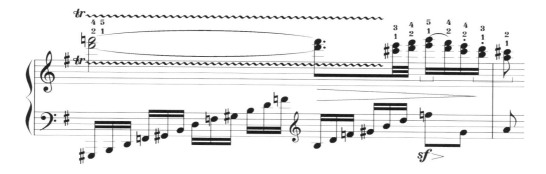

Here is the last example for the use of the thumb instead of finger 3 when played along with the little finger in scales in double thirds. It is the RH passage from Brahms, *Concerto No. 1*, first movement, measures 38-39 of the second theme.

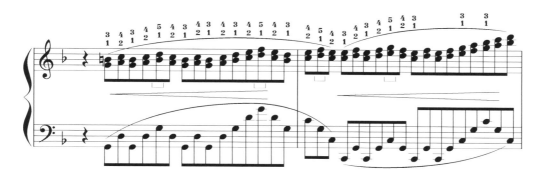

Here is another suggestion of a finger exercise for playing double thirds. It is based on the last extra fingering ideas as well as some new ones to be discussed later on. The exercise is shown in contrary motion, so it can easily be played hands together.

All of these ideas can serve the rest of the scales as well. Obviously, not every fingering discussed above is ideal for every scale, but there is enough variety to choose from, while mixing and matching of the fingering position groups will also be beneficial.

Fingering suggestions for two-octave scales will usually cover both multiple-octave scales and single-octave scales, the latter normally being shown in the second octave of the scale.

G major RH two octaves ascending:
1\2-1\3-2\4-3\5-1\3-2\4-3\5-1\2-1\3-2\4-3\5-1\2-1\3-2\4-3\5(or 1\5).
Return with the same fingering in reverse order.

G major LH two octaves ascending:
5\3(or 5\1)-4\2-3\1-2\1-5\3-4\2-3\1-5\3-4\2-3\1-2\1-5\3-4\2-3\1-2\1.
Return with the same fingering in reverse order. However, with this fingering, if the LH needs to turn around and return with no stop and no repetition of the last pair of notes, it means that we play 3\1-2\1 on the last two pairs of notes, and immediately change direction and play 3\1 again on the way down. We would be better off avoiding this move of the thumb – twice in a row, and in different directions. In this case we can use any of the following three fingerings:
   5\3(or 5\1)-4\2-3\1-2\1-5\3-4\2-3\1-5\3-4\2-3\1-5\3-4\2-3\1-4\2-3\1,
or 5\3(or 5\1)-4\2-3\1-5\3-4\2-3\1-2\1-5\3-4\2-3\1-5\3-4\2-3\1-4\2-3\1,
or 5\3(or 5\1)-4\2-3\1-2\1-5\3-4\2-3\1-2\1-5\3-4\2-3\1-4\2-3\1-4\2-3\1. Each of the above three fingerings can be used in reverse order for the descending return.

D major RH two octaves ascending:
1\2-1\3-2\4-3\5-1\3-2\4-3\5-1\2-1\3-2\4-3\5-1\2-1\3-2\4-3\5(or 1\5).
Return with the same fingering in reverse order.

D major LH two octaves ascending:
5\3-4\2-3\1-2\1-5\3-4\2-3\1-5\3-4\2-3\1-2\1-5\3-4\2-3\1-4\2.
Return with the same fingering in reverse order.

Switching the order of the two fingering groups 1\2-1\3-2\4-3\5 and 1\3-2\4-3\5 is optional when we play scales with white keys or scales with mostly white keys. This means that, instead of 1\2-1\3-2\4-3\5-1\3-2\4-3\5,

we can do 1\3-2\4-3\5-1\2-1\3-2\4-3\5, and vice versa, but context can help us determine the best order.

In Brahms, *Concerto No. 2*, last movement, measures 266-267, the famous RH ascending D major double-thirds scale, either of the following fingerings would work: 1\2-1\3-2\4-3\5-1\3-2\4-3\5, or switching around the order of the two fingering groups: 1\3-2\4-3\5-1\2-1\3-2\4-3\5. However, in measure 363 we have a similar passage which comes after the double-thirds trill D\F♯ and E♭\G in measure 362. We would normally play this double-thirds trill with fingers 1\3-2\4 or 1\3-2\5.

Moving from this double-thirds trill directly to the double-thirds scale would be better served if we start the double-thirds scale with fingers 1\3, which means that we use this fingering: 1\3-2\4-3\5-1\2-1\3-2\4-3\5.

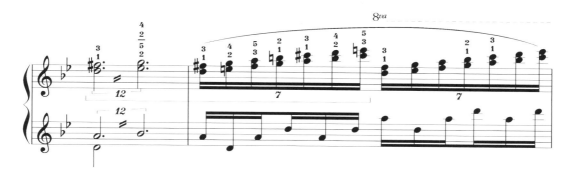

Since there are two good fingerings for this passage, some people may choose to use the same fingering for all similar occurrences of the ascending D major double-thirds scales in the RH rather than different fingerings at different spots. In general, both the same and different fingerings for similar passages have their own advantages. One advantage of doing the same fingering for similar passages is that we do not need to learn and practice two different fingerings. One advantage of doing different fingerings for similar passages is that it will help us with memorization. Different fingerings for similar passages will remind us that we are playing different spots in the piece.

In this particular D major double-thirds RH passage, as in some other double-thirds passages, some pianists choose to eliminate a note, or two, or even three in every octave, for an easier execution. This practice is known as one of the various "cheating" tricks that pianists may choose to employ when appropriate. If the tempo is very fast, this elimination of notes can hardly, if at all, be heard. The eliminated notes would most likely be chosen from the bottom notes of the thirds for acoustical, musical, and fingering considerations. If we want to eliminate one note when using this fingering 1\2-1\3-2\4-3\5-1\3-2\4-3\5 for the D major double-thirds scale, it would probably be best to eliminate the note E which is played by the thumb in the second pair of the fingering, after moving from D in the first pair.

If we want to eliminate a second and third note, perhaps finger 3 in the fourth and seventh pairs, where it plays on G and on C♯ respectively, will be a good choice. The reason for choosing finger 3 in these pairs is because it has very difficult tasks to achieve which may be impossible at a very high speed. What finger 3 needs to do for the first three times it plays in the scale is: be raised from the note G, play G again, be raised again from G and immediately go to C♯, an interval of an augmented fourth, while crossing over finger 5. Here is what this scale will look like after eliminating three notes in every octave.

Using the other fingering 1\3-2\4-3\5-1\2-1\3-2\4-3\5, we could eliminate the note A which is played by the thumb in the fifth pair of the fingering after moving from G in the fourth pair. The advantage of this particular note-elimination strategy is that, while we leave out the note A, at almost exactly the same time there is an A being played by the left hand.

Some people suggest eliminating even more notes as shown in the following example.

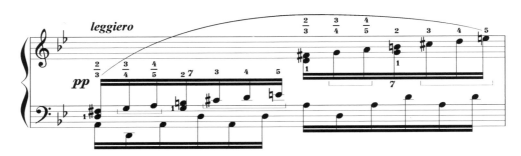

Good old redistribution can help the above passage as well. We can take with the LH every D and every G from the bottom notes of the thirds in the RH as shown in the next example.

Following are two more examples of note-elimination possibilities.

Beethoven, *Concerto No. 4*, first movement, measure 110 (measure 18 of the second *Solo* entrance), the *nachschlag* of the double-thirds trill can be done without the bottom note C♯, or even without the bottom two notes C♯ and D.

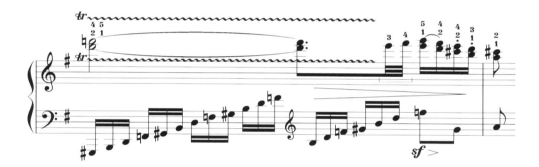

In Beethoven, *Concerto No. 5 (the Emperor)*, first movement, measure 12 of the third *Solo* after the orchestral introduction, and in other similar places, it is the C at the top of the fourth pair of notes that can be eliminated to allow an easier yet very crisp execution of this passage. This C has to be played with finger 3, and it is not easy coming from and going back to finger 4 on D. The explanation for choosing to eliminate it over any other note is that it appears two notes earlier and two notes later as the bottom note of the respective pairs of notes. So, even if it is left out as part of the fourth pair of notes, it still gets a good representation in the listener's ear, and eliminating it is hardly noticeable.

A major RH two octaves ascending:

1\3-2\4-3\5-1\2-1\3-2\4-3\5-1\3-2\4-3\5-1\2-1\3-2\4-3\5-1\4.

Return with the same fingering in reverse order.

A major LH two octaves ascending:

5\3-4\2-3\1-5\3-4\2-3\1-2\1-5\3-4\2-3\1-5\3-4\2-3\1-2\1-4\2(or 5\3).

Return with the same fingering in reverse order or see the next possibility. The pair of fingers 2\4 can act as a bridge between two fingering groups when ascending in the RH and when descending in the LH. An example for the RH ascending would look like this (the 2\4 fingering bridge is underlined): 1\3-2\4-3\5-2\4-1\3-2\4-3\5. Therefore, here is another useful possibility for A major LH two octaves descending: 4\2-3\1-4\2-5\3-4\2-3\1-4\2-5\3-2\1-3\1-4\2-5\3-3\1-4\2-5\3.

We have already discussed "odd" pairs of fingers, like 1\5 and 1\2, but there are other such useful "odd" pairs of fingers like 2\3, 2\5, and 1\4. We already saw the latter put to use at the top end of A major, RH. The next example will use some of these "odd" pairs of fingers (shown underlined).

E major RH two octaves ascending:

1\3-2\4-3\5-1\2-1\3-2\4-3\5-1\3-2\4-3\5-1\2-1\3-2\4-3\5-1\4. Return with the same fingering in reverse order. If we need to immediately turn around and go down without repeating the last pair of notes, we might want to consider descending with this fingering: 1\4-2\3-1\5-2\4-1\3-3\5-2\4-1\3-3\5-2\4-1\3-1\2-3\5-2\4-1\3.

Sometimes we may need to start with other than the first pair of fingers in a fingering group. **E major LH** ascending is an example of it. Though we can actually start at the beginning of the fingering group, when we get to the second octave we will realize that the fingering pair (underlined) for the notes E\G♯ is not the first pair of the group: 5\3-4\2-3\1-5\3-4\2-3\1-5\3-4\2-3\1-2\1-5\3-4\2-3\1-5\3-4\2 (or end with 4\2-3\1). Return with the same fingering in reverse order.

As we already saw before, using different fingerings for ascending and descending may be useful too, especially when playing more than a single octave. In **B major RH** we can use the same fingering for both ascending and descending if we use the traditional fingering which includes the two position groups of fingers 1\3-2\4-3\5 and 1\3-2\4. But if we want to reduce the number of crossings, and use larger position groups for greater speed and a lighter touch, we might be better off using different fingerings for each direction. This may also mean using different fingerings for each octave.

Ascending: 1\3-2\4-3\5-1\3-2\4-3\5-1\2-1\3-2\4-3\5-1\3-2\4-3\5-1\3-2\4.

Descending: 2\4-1\3-3\5-2\4-1\3-3\5-2\4-1\3-3\5-2\4-1\3-1\2-3\5-2\4-1\3.

These different fingerings for each direction enable the thumb to slide from a black key to a white one. This move is much smoother than having to "slide" from a white key to a black one, which is what we would have to do if we kept the ascending fingering in reverse order on the way down.

The same idea can serve the **B major LH**. Also notice that even though we will start ascending with the first pair of fingerings in the group, the "real" fingering is revealed only in the second octave (underlined).

Ascending: 5\3-4\2-3\1-5\3-4\2-3\1-5\3-<u>4\2</u>-3\1-5\3-4\2-3\1-2\1-4\2-3\1.

Descending: 3\1-4\2-3\1-4\2-5\3-2\1-3\1-4\2-5\3-3\1-4\2-5\3-3\1-4\2-5\3.

There is also the following possibility for the LH descending, although it puts the thumb on one extra black key in the two-octave scale:

3\1-4\2-3\1-4\2-5\3-3\1-4\2-5\3-2\1-3\1-4\2-5\3-3\1-4\2-5\3.

The idea of repeatedly using the full five-finger position group 1\3-2\4-3\5 in both hands can also apply here, though in the RH it will put the thumb on more black keys than the previous fingering. It will also have different fingerings for each octave, which is its nature, but it will keep the same fingering in both directions.

Based on ideas conveyed before, **F♯ major RH** two octaves ascending can be done as follows: 1\3-2\4-1\3-2\4-3\5-1\2-1\3-2\4-3\5-1\3-2\4-3\5-1\3-2\4-3\5.

RH descending: 3\5-2\4-1\3-3\5-2\4-1\3-1\2-3\5-2\4-1\3-3\5-2\4-1\3-2\4-1\3.

F♯ major LH two octaves

ascending: 4\2-3\1-5\3-4\2-3\1-5\3-4\2-3\1-2\1-5\3-4\2-3\1-5\3-4\2-3\1.

LH descending: 3\1-4\2-5\3-3\1-4\2-5\3-3\1-4\2-5\3-2\1-3\1-4\2-5\3-3\1-4\2.

C♯ major RH two octaves ascending can be the same as F♯ major:

1\3-2\4-1\3-2\4-3\5-1\2-1\3-2\4-3\5-1\3-2\4-3\5-1\3-2\4-3\5,

or as follows: 1\3-2\4-1\3-2\4-3\5-1\3-2\4-3\5-1\2-1\3-2\4-3\5-1\3-2\4-3\5.

RH descending: 3\5-2\4-1\3-3\5-2\4-1\3-3\5-2\4-1\3-3\5-2\4-1\3-1\2-2\4-1\3,

or: 2\4-1\3-3\5-2\4-1\3-1\2-3\5-2\4-1\3-3\5-2\4-1\3-1\2-2\4-1\3.

C♯ major LH two octaves ascending:

4\2-3\1-5\3-4\2-3\1-5\3-4\2-3\1-5\3-4\2-3\1-2\1-5\3-4\2-3\1.

LH descending: 3\1-4\2-5\3-3\1-4\2-5\3-2\1-3\1-4\2-5\3-3\1-4\2-5\3-3\1-4\2.

F major RH two octaves ascending:

2\4(or 1\2)-1\3-2\4-3\5-1\2-1\3-2\4-3\5-1\3-2\4-3\5-1\2-1\3-2\4-3\5.

Return with the same fingering in reverse order,

or: 3\5-2\4-1\3-1\2-3\5-2\4-1\3-1\2-3\5-2\4-1\3-3\5-2\4-1\3-2\4(or 1\2).

F major LH two octaves ascending:

5\3(or 5\1)-4\2-3\1-4\2-3\1-4\2-3\1-5\3-4\2-3\1-4\2-3\1-4\2-3\1-4\2(or 2\1),

or: 5\3(or 5\1)-4\2-3\1-4\2-3\1-4\2-3\1-5\3-4\2-3\1-4\2-3\1-5\3-4\2-3\1,

or: 4\1-5\3-4\2-3\1-2\1-5\3-4\2-3\1-5\3-4\2-3\1-2\1-5\3-4\2-3\1,

or: 5\3(or 5\1)-4\2-3\1-2\1-5\3-4\2-3\1-2\1-5\3-4\2-3\1-2\1-5\3-4\2-3\1.

LH descending: 3\1-4\2-5\3-2\1-3\1-4\2-5\3-3\1-4\2-5\3-2\1-3\1-4\2-5\3-4\1,

or: 3\1-4\2-5\3-2\1-3\1-4\2-5\3-2\1-3\1-4\2-5\3-2\1-3\1-4\2-5\3(or 5\1).

B♭ major RH two octaves ascending:
2\4(or 1\2)-1\3-2\4-3\5-1\2-1\3-2\4-3\5-1\3-2\4-3\5-1\2-1\3-2\4-3\5.
RH descending: 3\5-2\4-1\3-1\2-3\5-2\4-1\3-3\5-2\4-1\3-1\2-3\5-2\4-1\3-2\4.
   B♭ major LH two octaves ascending:
4\1-5\3-4\2-3\1-2\1-5\3-4\2-3\1-5\3-4\2-3\1-2\1-5\3-4\2-3\1,
or: 5\3(or 5\1)-4\2-3\1-2\1-5\3-4\2-3\1-2\1-5\3-4\2-3\1-2\1-5\3-4\2-3\1.
LH descending: 3\1-4\2-5\3-2\1-3\1-4\2-5\3-3\1-4\2-5\3-2\1-3\1-4\2-5\3-4\1,
or: 3\1-4\2-5\3-2\1-3\1-4\2-5\3-2\1-3\1-4\2-5\3-2\1-3\1-4\2-5\3(or 5\1).

   E♭ major RH two octaves ascending:
2\4(or 3\5)-1\2-1\3-2\4-3\5-1\3-2\4-3\5-1\2-1\3-2\4-3\5-1\3-2\4-3\5,
or: 1\3-2\4-1\3-2\4-3\5-1\3-2\4-3\5-1\2-1\3-2\4-3\5-1\3-2\4-3\5. Return with the same fingering in reverse order. Another possibility for E♭ major RH ascending is with the 2\4 bridging pair of fingers (underlined):
2\4(or 1\2)-1\3-2\4-3\5-<u>2\4</u>-1\3-2\4-3\5-1\3-2\4-3\5-<u>2\4</u>-1\3-2\4-3\5.
Return as before.
   E♭ major LH two octaves ascending:
4\1-5\3-4\2-3\1-2\1-5\3-4\2-3\1-5\3-4\2-3\1-2\1-5\3-4\2-3\1. Return in reverse order.

   A♭ major RH two octaves ascending:
1\3-2\4-1\3-2\4-3\5-1\2-1\3-2\4-3\5-1\3-2\4-3\5-1\3-2\4-3\5. Return in reverse order.
   A♭ major LH two octaves ascending (same as E♭ major):
4\1-5\3-4\2-3\1-2\1-5\3-4\2-3\1-5\3-4\2-3\1-2\1-5\3-4\2-3\1. Return with the same fingering in reverse order, or with the 4\2 bridging pair of fingers (underlined):
3\1-4\2-5\3-3\1-4\2-5\3-<u>4\2</u>-3\1-4\2-5\3-3\1-4\2-5\3-<u>4\2</u>-5\1.

All these principles, observations, and suggestions are as applicable for the minor scales. Natural minor scales may work well with the new fingering ideas while melodic and harmonic ones may benefit more from combining both the new and the traditional ideas, which may mean more finger crossings.

The harmonic minor scales will be discussed and given specific fingerings in the next paragraphs. Fingerings for the natural and melodic minor scales are pretty similar to the harmonic ones. In the cases that they are not, they can be figured out with the help of everything discussed both above and below. Another way of figuring out fingerings for the natural minor scales is simply playing their relative major scales with their own outlined fingerings and starting on the sixth note of the scale instead of on the tonic.

   A minor harmonic RH two octaves ascending:
1\3-2\4-3\5-1\2-1\3-2\4-3\5-1\2-1\3-2\4-3\5-1\2-1\3-2\4-1\5. Return in reverse order.
   A minor harmonic LH two octaves ascending:
5\3-4\2-3\1-2\1-5\3-4\2-3\1-5\3-4\2-3\1-2\1-5\3-4\2-3\1-4\2. Return in reverse order.

Remember that it is possible to slide with a finger from a black key to the adjacent white one instead of having to do an uncomfortable crossing. This can be done even with a pair of fingers on a pair of notes simultaneously, and it is particularly helpful if we are in a turning point where we need to change the scale direction and go back immediately.

E minor harmonic RH two octaves ascending (with a sliding finger underlined):
1\3-2\4-3\5-1\2-1\3-2\4-3\5-1\3-2\4-3\5-1\2-1\3-2\4-3\5-1\5,
or: 1\3-2\4-3\5-1\2-1\3-2\4-3\5-1\5-2\3-1\4-2\5-1\3-2\4-3\5-1\5.
RH descending: 1\5-2\4-1\3-1\2-3\5-2\4-1\3-1\2-3\5-2\4-1\3-1\2-3\5-2\4-1\3.
E minor harmonic LH two octaves ascending:
4\2-3\1-5\3-4\2-3\1-2\1-5\3-4\2-3\1-2\1-5\3-4\2-3\1-4\2-3\1. Sometimes it might be better to use this three-pair group 1\2-1\3-2\4 (underlined in the example) instead of the common group 1\3-2\4-3\5. This can be good for either hand in either direction. Therefore, here is another possibility for E minor Harmonic LH two octaves ascending: 5\3(or 5\1)-4\2-3\1-2\1-5\3-4\2-3\1-2\1-4\2-3\1-2\1-4\2-3\1-4\2-3\1. And yet another possibility for E minor Harmonic LH two octaves ascending that employs a pair of fingers sliding from black keys to white ones (underlined in the example): 5\3(or 5\1)-4\2-3\1-2\1-5\3-4\2-3\1-2\1-4\2-3\1-2\1-5\3-4\2-3\1-3\1. Of course we can finish this last fingering with 3\1-2\1, but the double-slide ending enables us to change direction and return without having to repeat the top end pair of notes and change fingering on it.
LH descending: 3\1-4\2-3\1-4\2-5\3-3\1-4\2-5\3-2\1-3\1-4\2-5\3-3\1-4\2-5\3(or 5\1).

B minor harmonic RH two octaves ascending, using some of the "odd" pairs of fingers, as well as the sliding tool (both types underlined):
1\3-2\4-1\3-2\4-3\5-1\5-2\3-1\4-2\5-1\3-2\4-3\5-1\5-2\3-1\5. B minor harmonic RH two octaves descending, where we will again see the use of this three-pair group 1\2-1\3-2\4 (underlined) instead of the common group 1\3-2\4-3\5:
1\5-2\4-1\3-2\4-1\3-2\4-1\3-1\2-3\5-2\4-1\3-1\2-2\4-1\3-1\2.
B minor harmonic LH two octaves ascending:
5\2-3\1-5\3-4\2-3\1-2\1-5\3-4\2-3\1-5\3-4\2-3\1-2\1-4\2-3\1.
LH descending: 3\1-4\2-5\3-2\1-3\1-4\2-5\3-3\1-4\2-5\3-2\1-3\1-4\2-3\1-5\2.

F♯ minor harmonic RH two octaves ascending:
1\3-2\4-1\3-2\4-3\5-1\3-2\4-3\5-2\4-1\3-2\4-3\5-1\3-2\4-3\5,
or: 1\3-2\4-1\3-2\4-3\5-1\2-1\3-2\4-3\5-1\3-2\4-3\5-1\3-2\4-3\5.
RH descending: 3\5-2\4-1\3-3\5-2\4-1\3-3\5-2\4-1\3-1\2-3\5-2\4-1\3-2\4-1\3.
F♯ minor harmonic LH two octaves ascending:
4\2-3\1-5\3-4\2-3\1-5\3-4\2-3\1-2\1-5\3-4\2-3\1-5\3-4\2-3\1. Return in reverse order.

C# minor harmonic RH two octaves ascending:
1\3-2\4-1\3-2\4-3\5-1\2-1\3-2\4-3\5-1\3-2\4-3\5-1\3-2\4-3\5. Return with the same fingering in reverse order. Another possibility for RH two octaves ascending:
1\3-2\4-1\3-2\4-3\5-1\3-2\4-3\5-1\2-1\3-2\4-3\5-1\3-2\4-3\5.
Another possibility for RH two octaves descending:
3\5-2\4-1\3-3\5-2\4-1\3-2\4-1\3-2\4-1\3-3\5-2\4-1\3-2\4-1\3.

C# minor harmonic LH two octaves ascending:
4\1-5\3-4\2-3\1-2\1-5\3-4\2-3\1-5\3-4\2-3\1-2\1-5\3-4\2-3\1.
LH descending: 3\1-4\2-5\3-3\1-4\2-5\3-2\1-3\1-4\2-5\3-3\1-4\2-5\3-4\2-5\1,
or: 3\1-4\2-5\3-3\1-4\2-5\3-4\2-3\1-4\2-5\3-3\1-4\2-5\3-4\2-5\1.

G# minor harmonic RH two octaves ascending:
1\3-2\4-1\3-2\4-3\5-1\3-2\4-3\5-1\2(or 2\4)-1\3-2\4-3\5-1\3-2\4-3\5.
RH descending: 3\5-2\4-1\3-3\5-2\4-1\3-3\5-2\4-1\3-1\2-3\5-2\4-1\3-2\4-1\3.

G# minor harmonic LH two octaves ascending (like C# minor):
4\1-5\3-4\2-3\1-2\1-5\3-4\2-3\1-5\3-4\2-3\1-2\1-5\3-4\2-3\1.
G# minor harmonic LH two octaves descending (like C# minor):
3\1-4\2-5\3-3\1-4\2-5\3-2\1(or 4\2)-3\1-4\2-5\3-3\1-4\2-5\3-4\2-5\1.

D# minor harmonic RH two octaves ascending:
1\2-1\3-2\4-3\5-2\4-1\3-2\4-3\5-1\3-2\4-3\5-2\4-1\3-2\4-3\5.
RH descending: 3\5-2\4-1\3-3\5-2\4-1\3-1\2-3\5-2\4-1\3-3\5-2\4-1\3-1\2-2\4.

D# minor harmonic LH two octaves ascending:
5\3-4\2-3\1-2\1-5\2-4\1-2\1-5\3-4\2-3\1-2\1-5\2-4\1-2\1-3\2.
LH descending: 3\2-4\1-5\2-3\1-4\2-3\1-4\2-3\1-4\1-5\2-3\1-4\2-3\1-4\2-5\3.

A# minor harmonic RH two octaves ascending:
1\3-2\4-3\5-1\2-1\3-2\4-3\5-1\3-2\4-3\5-1\2-1\3-2\4-1\5-2\4.
A# minor harmonic RH two octaves descending:
2\4-1\5-2\4-1\5(or 1\3)-2\4-1\3-1\2-2\4-1\5-2\4-1\5(or 1\3)-2\4-1\3-1\2-2\4,
or: 2\4-1\5-2\4-1\5-2\4-1\3-1\2-3\5-2\4-1\3-1\2-3\5-2\4-1\3-2\4,
or: 2\4-2\5-1\3-1\2-3\5-2\4-1\3-2\4-2\5-1\3-1\2-3\5-2\4-1\3-2\4,
or: 2\4-2\5-1\3-1\2-3\5-2\4-1\3-5\3-2\4-1\3-1\2-3\5-2\4-1\3-2\4.

A# minor harmonic LH two octaves ascending:
5\3-4\2-3\1-5\3-4\2-3\1-2\1-5\3-4\2-3\1-5\3-4\2-3\1-2\1-4\2(or 3\2).
A# minor harmonic LH two octaves descending:
4\2(or 3\2)-3\1-4\2-5\3-2\1(or 4\2)-3\1-4\2-5\3-3\1-4\2-5\3-2\1(or 4\2)-3\1-4\2-5\3.

D minor harmonic RH two octaves ascending:
1\3-2\4-3\5-1\2-1\3-2\4-3\5-1\3-2\4-3\5-1\2-1\3-2\4-3\5-1\4. Return in reverse order.
Another ascending possibility:
1\3-2\4-3\5-1\2-1\3-2\4-3\5-1\3-2\4-3\5-1\3-2\4-3\5-2\4-1\5.

RH descending: 1\5-2\4-1\3-1\2-2\4-1\3-2\4-1\3-3\5-2\4-1\3-1\2-3\5-2\4-1\3,
or: 1\5-2\4-1\3-1\2-2\4-1\3-1\2-3\5-2\4-1\3-1\2-2\4-1\3-2\4-1\3.
D minor harmonic LH two octaves ascending:
5\3(or 5\1)-4\2-3\1-5\3-4\2-3\1-2\1-5\3-4\2-3\1-5\3-4\2-3\1-4\2-3\1,
or: 5\3(or 5\1)-4\2-3\1-5\3-4\2-3\1-2\1-4\2-3\1-2\1-5\3-4\2-3\1-4\2-3\1.
Return with the same fingerings in reverse order.

G minor harmonic RH two octaves ascending (like D minor):
1\3-2\4-3\5-1\2-1\3-2\4-3\5-1\3-2\4-3\5-1\2-1\3-2\4-3\5-1\4. Return in reverse order.
G minor harmonic LH two octaves ascending (like D minor):
5\3-4\2-3\1-5\3-4\2-3\1-2\1-5\3-4\2-3\1-5\3-4\2-3\1-4\2-3\1 (or end with 2\1-4\2 if not returning with the same fingering). Return with the same fingering in reverse order, or: 4\2-3\1-4\2-5\3-4\2-3\1-4\2-5\3-3\1-4\2-5\3-4\2-3\1-4\2-5\3,
or: 4\2-3\1-4\2-5\3-4\2-3\1-4\2-5\3-2\1-3\1-4\2-5\3-3\1-4\2-5\3.

C minor harmonic RH two octaves ascending (like D minor and G minor):
1\3-2\4-3\5-1\2-1\3-2\4-3\5-1\3-2\4-3\5-1\2-1\3-2\4-3\5-1\4. Return in reverse order.
C minor harmonic LH two octaves ascending (like D minor and G minor):
5\3-4\2-3\1-5\3-4\2-3\1-2\1-5\3-4\2-3\1-5\3-4\2-3\1-4\2-3\1. Return in reverse order.

F minor harmonic RH two octaves ascending:
1\2-1\3-2\4-3\5-1\3-2\4-3\5-1\2-1\3-2\4-3\5-1\3-2\4-3\5-1\4. Return in reverse order.
The above RH ascending fingering is not the best for *legato* because of the transition from the pair of notes B♭\D♭ with fingers 3\5 to the next pair C\E with fingers 1\3 (both fingering pairs underlined). However, when this transition is reversed in descending, the legato is smoother. The following RH ascending fingering, used also for the minor scales D, G, and C, offers a better *legato* for the F minor harmonic two octaves: 1\3-2\4-3\5-1\2-1\3-2\4-3\5-1\3-2\4-3\5-1\2-1\3-2\4-3\5-1\4.
Return by reversing the first fingering.
F minor harmonic LH two octaves ascending (like the minor scales D, G, and C): 5\3-4\2-3\1-5\3-4\2-3\1-2\1-5\3-4\2-3\1-5\3-4\2-3\1-4\2-3\1.
Return with the same fingering in reverse order.

Note: Many of the scales which were given specific and multiple fingerings may still have even more fingering possibilities. The fingering discussed and suggested above may still need to be modified, as the real music may not necessarily follow the scale examples as they appear here – or anywhere else for that matter. The understanding of the double fingering groups and how they work will be of great help in solving these fingering puzzles.

Chromatic scales in double thirds

The choice here is between two principles: The old-school fingering that utilizes the move of the thumb between two adjacent white keys and the modern fingering utilizing the tool of sliding finger 2 from a black key to an adjacent white key. I prefer the modern fingering, as I view the slide from a black key to a white one a better move than a "slide" between two white keys. The principle in both hands ascending is that the second finger slides from D♯ to E and from A♯ to B. In both hands descending, the principle is that the second finger slides from D♭ to C and from G♭ to F. These principles are good for both major and minor double thirds.

RH descending chromatic minor double-thirds fingering starting on D\F:
1\5-2\4-2\3-1\4-2\3-1\5-2\4-1\3-2\4-2\3-1\4-2\3,
or: 1\5-2\4-2\3-1\5-2\4-1\5-2\4-1\3-2\4-2\3-1\5-2\4. For the LH ascending, we mirror it and start on B\D: 5\1-4\2-3\2-4\1-3\2-5\1-4\2-3\1-4\2-3\2-4\1-3\2,
or: 5\1-4\2-3\2-5\1-4\2-5\1-4\2-3\1-4\2-3\2-5\1-4\2.

RH ascending chromatic minor double-thirds fingering starting on C\E♭:
1\3-2\4-1\5-2\3-2\4-1\3-2\4-1\3-2\4-1\5-2\3-2\4,
or: 1\3-2\4-1\5-2\4-2\5-1\3-2\4-1\3-2\4-1\5-2\4-2\5. For the LH descending, we mirror it and start on C♯\E: 3\1-4\2-5\1-3\2-4\2-3\1-4\2-3\1-4\2-5\1-3\2-4\2,
or: 3\1-4\2-5\1-4\2-5\2-3\1-4\2-3\1-4\2-5\1-4\2-5\2.

The Romantic-period literature is very fond of using these flashy passages. Following are two RH examples: Grieg, *Concerto in A minor*, first movement, measure 41 for descending chromatic minor thirds, and Saint-Saëns, *Concerto No. 4 in C minor*, first movement, measure 157 for ascending chromatic minor thirds.

Chromatic major double thirds are especially favored by Liszt. Following is his *Transcendental Etude No. 4 – Mazeppa*, measure 100 (15 measures before the time signature changes to six eighths).

Scales in double fourths

We usually use either 1\4-2\5 or 2\4-1\5. The fingering 2\4-1\5 can produce a better *legato* when playing more than just two double fourths in a scale. A more creative fingering like 1\3-2\4-3\5, or even 1\2-1\3-2\4-3\5, can also be used. Following is a suggested exercise with three different fingerings as shown separated by two long horizontal lines. The exercise is not necessarily meant to be played hands together, though it is possible. However, if one decides to play the exercise with both hands together, I would suggest mixing and matching the fingerings.

We can also employ the tool of sliding from black to white keys as well as the tool of redistribution. Either of these tools can be of great help, when appropriate.

In the first movement of Chopin, *Sonata No. 3, Op. 58 in B minor*, measure 20, the right hand has a descending double-fourths scale. This passage can be fingered in many different ways, from the simplest straightforward fingering 2\5-1\4 throughout, to more creative fingerings. The following two examples show several different ways of fingering this passage.

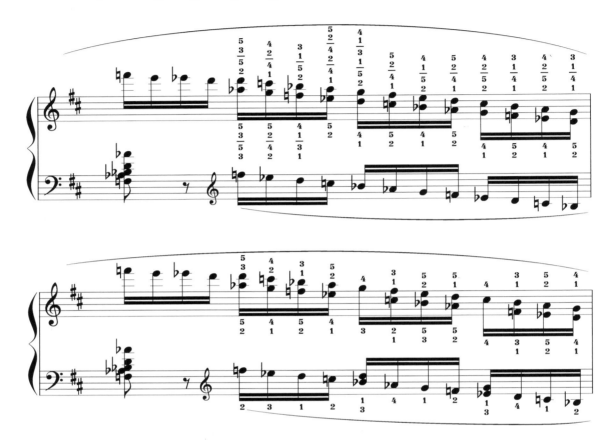

Chromatic scales in double fourths

The principle of sliding the second finger from black keys to their adjacent white ones, as mentioned in chromatic double thirds, is also very helpful here. However, here we add another sliding finger from the same black keys. When ascending, finger 4 (in addition to finger 2) in both hands will also slide from D♯ to E and from A♯ to B. When descending, finger 4 in both hands will slide from D♭ to C and from G♭ to F.

RH descending chromatic fourths fingering starting on D♭\G♭:
2\4-2\4-1\5-2\4-1\5-2\4-1\4-2\5-2\4-1\5-2\4-1\5. LH ascending chromatic fourths fingering starting on A♯\D♯: 4\2-4\2-5\1-4\2-5\1-4\2-4\1-5\2-4\2-5\1-4\2-5\1.

RH ascending chromatic fourths fingering starting on A♯\D♯:
2\4-2\4-1\5-2\4-1\5-2\4-2\5-1\4-2\4-1\5-2\4-1\5. LH descending chromatic fourths fingering starting on D♭\G♭: 4\2-4\2-5\1-4\2-5\1-4\2-5\2-4\1-4\2-5\1-4\2-5\1.

In the *Scherzo* of Chopin, *Sonata No. 2, Op. 35 in B♭ minor*, measures 37-39, the right hand has an ascending double-fourths chromatic scale.

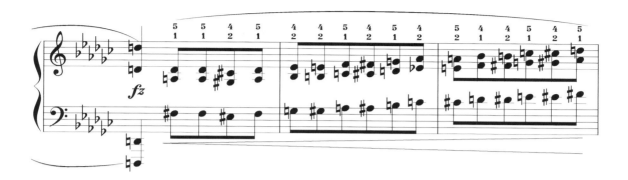

Scales in double fifths

Using fingers 2 and 4 together for playing a fifth is possible, but for some people it might be too much of a stretch on the white keys, let alone on the two fifths that span from B♭ to F, and from B to F♯. Therefore the best fingering would be 1\4-2\5. Sometimes, depending on the demands of the text, we may choose to use 1\2-1\3-1\4-1\5. A judicious merging of the above two fingering suggestions can also work well: 1\2-1\3-1\4-2\5. Following are a couple of double-fifths exercises; the first one has two fingerings. Though it is possible, there is no need to play the two hands together.

Of course, the tool of sliding from black to white keys is always good too. Due to counterpoint and harmony rules, double-fifths scales are not something we would encounter often, if at all, in traditional classical music. My own *Rhapsody in Blue*

and White does have these parallel fifths, though not in *legato*. The only *legato* between adjacent parallel fifths in my *Rhapsody* is a chromatic move from two black keys to two white keys, as will be discussed in "Chromatic scales in double fifths". Here are measures 95-97 of my *Rhapsody* with my fingerings for both the *legato* and the *non-legato* executions of the double fifths.

Chromatic scales in double fifths

Fingers 2 and 4 together would be useful here on the black keys, as we saw in the last example. Some people may also choose to use them on the white keys' stretches. We can play an ascending chromatic scale in double fifths with the following fingering for the RH, starting on C\G: 1\5-2\4-1\5-2\4-2\5-1\5-2\4-1\5-2\4-1\5-2\5-1\4-2\5 (or 1\5 when continuing another octave). For a very large-span hand: 1\5-2\4-1\5-2\4-2\4-1\5-2\4-1\5-2\4-1\4-2\5-2\4-1\5. LH descending can use the mirrored fingering starting on A\E: 5\1-4\2-5\1-4\2-5\2-5\1-4\2-5\1-4\2-5\1-5\2-4\1-5\2 (or 5\1 when continuing another octave). For a very large-span hand: 5\1-4\2-5\1-4\2-4\2-5\1-4\2-5\1-4\2-4\1-5\2-4\2-5\1.

RH descending, starting on C\G: 2\5-1\4-2\5 (or 2\4 for a very large-span hand) -1\5-2\4-1\5-2\4-2\5 (or 2\4 for a large-span hand) -1\5-2\4-1\5-2\4-1\5 (or 2\5 when continuing another octave). LH ascending can use the mirrored fingering starting on A\E: 5\2-4\1-5\2 (or 4\2 for a very large-span hand) -5\1-4\2-5\1-4\2-5\2 (or 4\2 for a large-span hand) -5\1-4\2-5\1-4\2-5\1 (or 5\2 when continuing another octave).

In a piano arrangement of Piazzolla's *Invierno Porteño, Winter* from *The Four Seasons of Buenos Aires,* measure 28, we find for the RH a descending chromatic scale of fifths in *legato*.

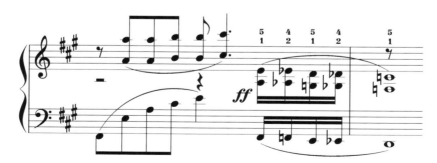

Scales in double sixths

Fingering here is pretty much the same as for double fifths: 1\4-2\5, or 1\2-1\3-1\4-1\5 and various combinations of the two sets, as well as sliding from black to white keys where appropriate.

Following is a double-sixths exercise with two fingerings.

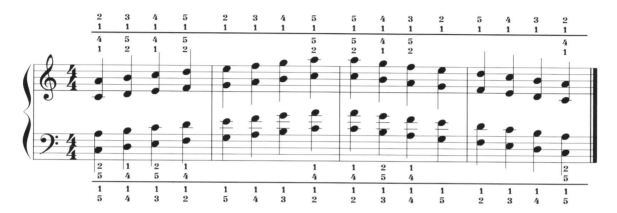

Three measures from the end of Chopin's *Nocturne in D♭ major Op. 27, No. 2* there is an ascending scale of sixths in the RH. Here is my suggested fingering for this passage.

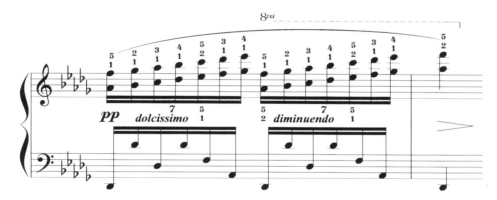

In Schubert's *Impromptu Op. 90, No. 1*, measure 77, we find a descending pentascale of sixths in the RH.

Chromatic scales in double sixths

The same fingering ideas as for diatonic scales in double sixths will serve us for chromatic scales in both major and minor double sixths.

The RH in Chopin's *Étude Op. 25, No. 8* has chromatic scales in both major and minor sixths. Measure 7 has the ascending major sixths.

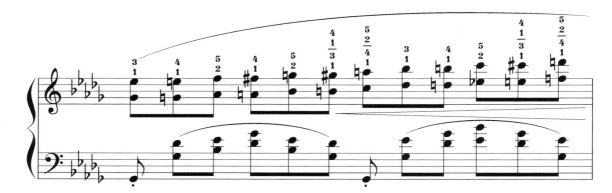

Measures 32-34 have the ascending minor sixths. The scale appears in three consecutive octaves, one octave per measure. The example will show just one octave – measure 32 (5 measures from the end). The optional use of fingers 2\4 on A♯\F♯ is obviously for a very large-span hand.

Scales in double octaves

A single octave can be played with the thumb at one end and finger 5, or 4, or 3, or even 2 at the other end. Some pianists prefer to use finger 4 on a black key and finger 5 on a white key. Some pianists also use fingers 4 and 5 together on the same key as if they are glued to each other. This practice may add the security of not sliding off to the wrong key, and it may also help to bring out top notes in the RH and bottom notes in the LH. Some pianists even use fingers 3, 4, and 5 together on one key. I would not recommend overdoing it with the use of the 3 last fingers together on one key, as the twist and the stretch can be harmful to the hands.

There are various techniques for playing fast *non-legato* double octaves:

1.   Using the entire forearm and hand (all the way from the elbow) as one unit that moves up and down is very powerful, but it could be harmful to the hands.

2.   I prefer pushing the forearm and hand into the keys as if there is something behind the elbow pushing it forward and releasing, back and forth.

3.   Slightly dipping the wrist with each played octave.

4.   There is the catching technique where the fingers close into the octave keys while facing each other and seizing the other keys between the two octave keys like a pair of tongs holding a block of ice.

5.   For the fastest *non-legato* double octaves with a little less power, there is the butterfly technique, where the hand moves from the wrist like a butterfly's wing. There are two schools of practicing and acquiring this technique:

a.) When the hand is up, keep the octave distance between fingers 1 and 5 unchanged like a claw. Here, opinions vary regarding the position of the three middle fingers. Some say to bend them quite tightly as to get them out of the way; others say to keep them unbent.

b.) When the hand is up, let all the fingers relax and flex naturally.

Sometimes, some of these octave techniques can be combined.

We cannot play octaves in a perfect *legato* articulation. The next best thing we can do is play only one of the two voices *legato* – the one not played with the thumb. For that *legato* voice we can repeatedly use fingers 4-5, or 3-4-5; exceptionally big hands with a large span can use fingers 2-3-4-5.

Suggested exercise in double octaves for small hands:

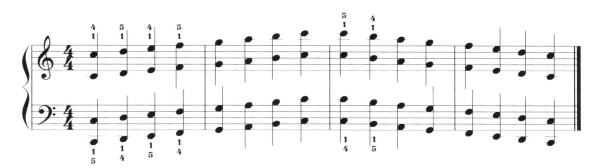

Suggested exercise in double octaves for medium size hands:

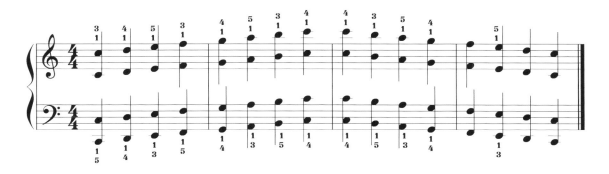

Suggested exercise in double octaves for big hands:

The next example shows how the double-octave fingering 1\3-1\4-1\5 can be put to good use and help with *legato* playing in the right hand. Chopin, *Prelude No. 24 in D minor*, 18 measures from the end:

Of course, sliding from a black key to the neighboring white one is always a good option too. The following example is the melody in octaves at the beginning of *Papillons Op. 2* by Schumann.

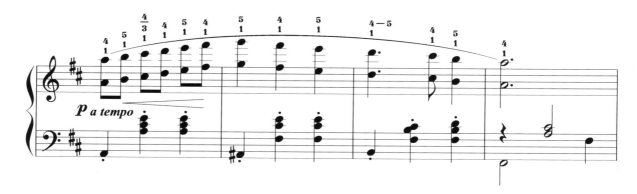

The famous *octave Étude Op. 25, No. 10* by Chopin calls for very *legato* playing in the middle section marked *Lento*. Here are a few fingering possibilities for measures 3-6 in this *Lento* section, all based on the use of the thumb at one end of the octave and a combination of fingers 3, 4, and 5 at the other end of the octave.

Chromatic scales in double octaves

The same fingering ideas for diatonic scales in double octaves are also good for chromatic scales in double octaves. The side of the octave that is not played with the thumb will usually have finger 4 on a black key and finger 5 on a white key, except when the black key precedes the group of two adjacent white keys in the ascending RH and in the descending LH, in which case, finger 3 will be on the black key, and fingers 4 and 5 on the two white keys.

The following example can also be used as an exercise.

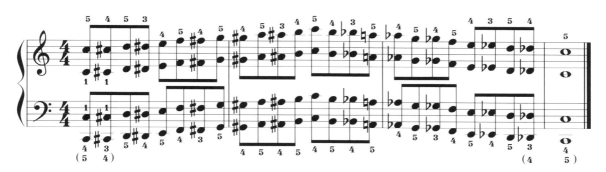

Let us look again at Chopin *Étude Op. 25, No. 10*, this time at the very beginning where both hands play chromatic passages in double octaves. Measures 1-2:

Allegro con fuoco.

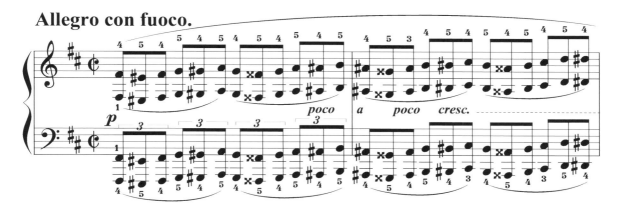

Variation No. 7 in Book I of the Brahms – Paganini *Variations* has a chromatic scale in one hand and a mix of both chromatic and diatonic scales in the other hand. This appears twice, and then the hands change roles as well as have variations on these scales. The following example will show measures 1 and 5.

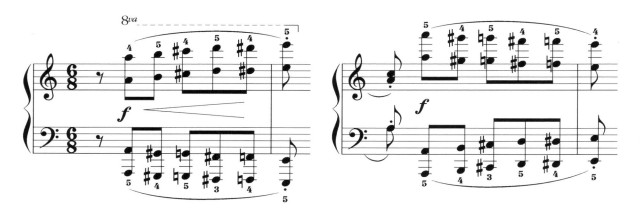

Octaves with an extra note inside

(Intervals are counted from the bottom note up.)

RH octave with a third inside: 1\2\5, on rare occasions 1\3\5.

RH octave with a fourth inside: 1\2\5, or 1\3\5, on rare occasions 1\2\4.

RH octave with a fifth inside: 1\3\5, or 1\2\5, or 1\2\4.

RH octave with a sixth inside: 1\3\5, or 1\4\5, or 1\2\4, on rare occasions 1\2\3, or 1\2\5.

LH octave with a third inside: 5\3\1, or 5\4\1, or 4\2\1, on rare occasions 3\2\1, or 5\2\1.

LH octave with a fourth inside: 5\3\1, or 5\2\1, or 4\2\1.

LH octave with a fifth inside: 5\2\1, or 5\3\1, on rare occasions 4\2\1.

LH octave with a sixth inside: 5\2\1, on rare occasions 5\3\1.

Just like octaves, the above chords cannot be played as a scale in a perfect *legato* articulation. Some of them can be played with a partial *legato*, where some of the chord voices can be *legato*.

A RH octave with a sixth inside and its mirror, a LH octave with a third inside, can be played in *non-legato* scales with 1\3\5. We can achieve a very partial *legato* with the fingering 1\3\5 and 1\4\5, as *legato* can be played between the fingers 3 and 4. We can achieve an even better *legato* with the fingering 1\2\4 and 1\3\5, as *legato* can be played between the fingers 2\4 and 3\5.

Following is an example/exercise with the two fingerings mentioned above. The hands are not meant to be played together.

Of course, a combination of the above two fingerings is a good possibility too. For example, we can start with the ascending RH fingers 1\2\4 going to 1\3\5 and then continue with 1\4\5. The same can be as good for the LH descending. We can start with 4\2\1 going to 5\3\1 and then continue with 5\4\1. This is shown in the next example/exercise.

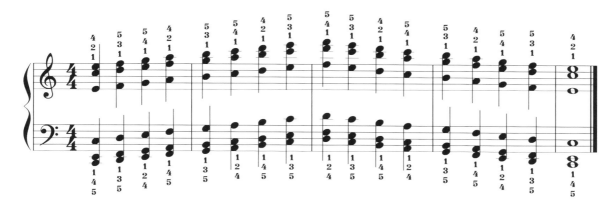

Three consecutive ascending RH octaves with a sixth inside can be fingered with 1\2\4-1\3\5-1\4\5, as we can see in the next example from Gershwin's *Rhapsody in Blue*. Measure 69 in the slow section marked *Andantino moderato con espressione*:

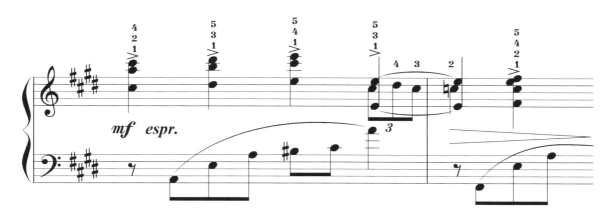

Another example is in Chopin's *Polonaise Fantaisie*. Here, a large-span hand can also use the fingering of 1\2\3 within the progression of these chords. Following are two fingering possibilities for these descending chord passages as they appear in measures 25-26 of the *a tempo primo* section.

Large-Span Chords, Rolled Chords, and Leaping Grace Notes

Large-span chords often need to be rolled. Such chords, and chords which are actually marked as rolled, whether written as chords or as grace notes, can be approached and fingered in a number of different ways:

1.   In one hand position with no finger crossings, as mostly required by Chopin's *Étude Op. 10, No. 11*. Here is just the first measure.

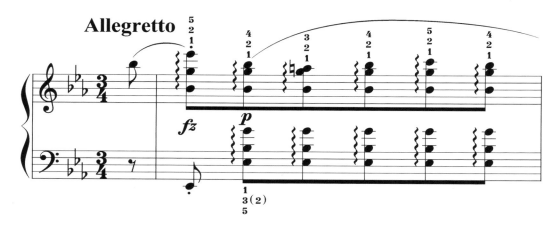

2.   With finger crossings to a new hand position, as we can see in Chopin's *Étude Op. 10, No. 8*, measure 15, first beat in the LH:

3. By rewriting it rhythmically. Let us look at Chopin's *Étude Op. 10, No. 5*, 21 measures from the end, first beat in the LH. The way it is originally written is quite impossible to play even for a big hand.

In order to be able to execute it we need to rewrite it. I suggest one of the next four possibilities, all with the same fingering, and with pedal starting from the octave grace notes in the bass.

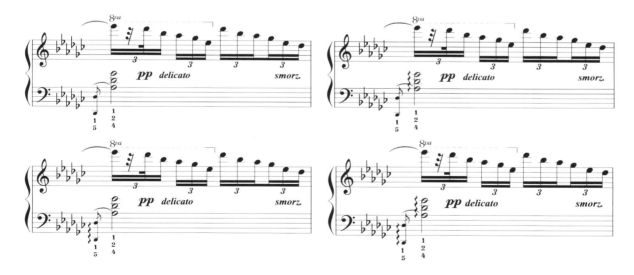

4. By rewriting it note-wise, which means moving a note to a more convenient octave within the chord. Busoni's transcription of Bach's organ piece

Toccata in C major, BWV 564 presents such an opportunity in measures 72-74 of the Fugue. Every third and sixth chord in these measures presents a challenge for the RH. This challenge intensifies at a faster tempo, and particularly so in the third chord of both measures 73 and 74. Having to play the chord C♯\F\C♯ and the chord D♯\G\D♯ with the RH fingers 1\3\5 is not a very healthy position and stretch for the hand. Originally written as follows:

Rewritten as follows:

Another example is at the end of Gershwin's *Rhapsody in Blue*. Thirteen and eleven measures from the end, we have major and minor tenths, respectively, in the LH as the frame of the rolled chords. Originally written as follows:

Some people may find it very hard to execute in tempo and in *fortissimo*. A solution could be to move only the bass note one octave higher. Even though it may sound a little different, we are still keeping all four notes in the chord, we can hold the pedal from the beginning of the measure where the "missing" bass note is played with an octave reinforcement, thus it will still be sounding. The orchestra also helps cover for the "missing" bass note by playing it four times in the same measure. Rewritten as follows:

5.   By using hand redistribution, where possible. Chopin's *Waltz in F major Op. 34, No. 3* starts with interlocking chords where the frame of the LH chord is a span of a major tenth, from C to E. Some hands cannot stretch that far, and must roll it, but this is not necessary if the top E in the LH is redistributed to the RH. Measures 1-4 as originally written:

Measures 1-4 with hands redistribution:

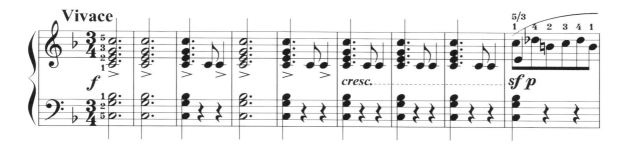

A similar chord is the second LH eighth note in measure 24 of Chopin's *Étude Op. 10, No. 7*. Also here it is possible to play with the RH the top note of the LH.

Another interlocking chord is the grace note leaping to the very last note of Chopin's *Scherzo No. 2, Op. 31*. The following example shows the original on the left and two other execution possibilities on the right.

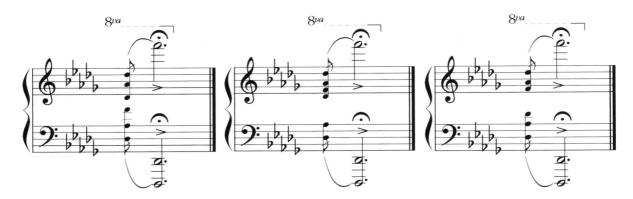

In *Tempo I* of *Nocturne Op. 15, No. 1* by Chopin, the RH has 3 grace notes as an arpeggio leading to the top main note. If played before the beat, the first grace note, which is the middle C, can be taken with the LH.

A similar case is the opening of Chopin's *Sonata No. 2*. In the third measure we can use the LH to play the first grace note written for the RH. The following example is shown with the redistribution of that grace note.

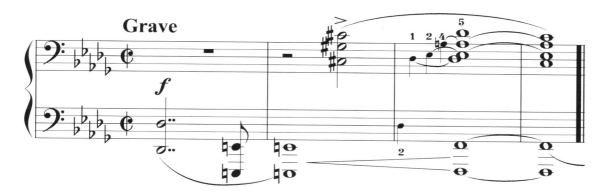

Another similar case is the RH grace notes in measure 89 of Chopin's *Scherzo No. 4, Op. 54*. Here I suggest taking the first two grace notes with the LH as shown in the next example.

6. By omitting a note if necessary. There are spots in Gershwin's *Rhapsody in Blue* where similarly spread, large rolled chords have to be played by the LH. The chords span a major tenth and contain the intervals of a fifth and an octave from the bass note. At a moderate speed and a medium dynamic, it is possible, even for a small hand, to play these rolled chords. However, these chords must be played loud and crisp, and must be rolled fast, almost sounding together, as they are up against a heavily orchestrated, full symphony score. This kind of environment may pose a problem for the small hand. I suggest that, by omitting one note, even the small hand can sound loud and crisp in these chords. Actually any of the four notes which are in the LH part of the chord can be omitted, as each one of them appears anyway in different octaves, both in the RH part of the same chord and in the orchestral part of the same chord. In the following three examples I chose to omit the top note of the rolled chord in the LH which is a tenth from the bass note. It is not necessarily the best choice, just a choice used to convey the idea. The suggested note to be omitted is marked with parenthesis and the fingering shown here is for the chord with the top note already omitted.

These three spots in the piece are as follows:

a.) Measure 81 in the *Solo* entrance:

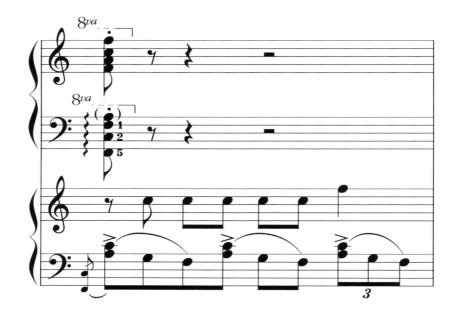

b.) The first measure in *Animato*:

c.) One measure from the end of the piece, the fourth chord:

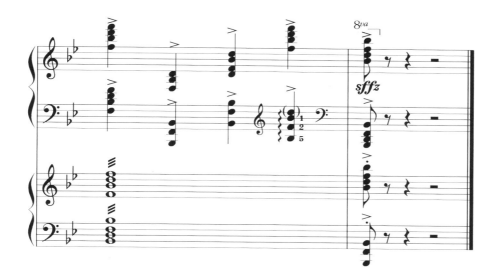

Large rolled chords and grace notes which are far from the main notes, such that even a large hand cannot block them together, tend to take extra time and distort good rhythm. They should be played fast, yet clear. There are many cases where there is no extra time to insert the grace note or the rolled notes of the chord between the beat and the preceding played note. A very useful solution for this problem is to start the grace note or the rolled chord as early as playing it together with the preceding note in the other hand. Ravel actually notates it this way in *Ondine* from *Gaspard de la Nuit*, e.g., measures 58 and 59. I added arrows to the score for the sake of clarity.

In most cases composers did not spell it out this way, and it is up to us to take advantage of this tool. Chopin's *Revolutionary Étude, Op. 10, No. 12* has a large RH rolled chord in the first beat of measure 55. The notes are A\D\A\D, spanning the interval of an 11th, while the LH plays fast sixteenth notes. It is quite hard, or even impossible for a small hand to fit the first three notes in the rolled chord before the beat without taking extra time. The solution here is to start the rolled chord with the last sixteenth note in the LH. The next example shows the rolled chord as it appears in the score, followed by the suggested solution.

Another example is the LH rolled chord in measure 45 of *The Lilacs Op. 21, No. 5* by Rachmaninov. Measures 44-45 as written originally:

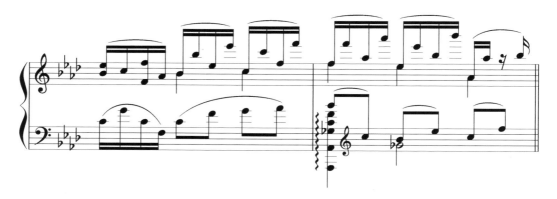

Measures 44-45 with the suggested solution:

The *Andante* from Schubert's *A minor Sonata Op. 143, D. 784*, has quite a few large-span, rolled chords in the LH. The following example will show measure 35, on the left as originally written, and on the right with my suggested solution.

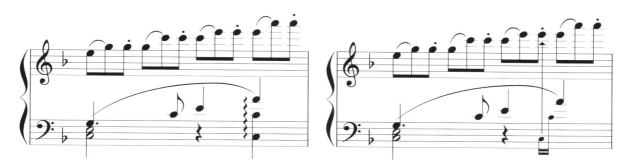

The *eighth Etude* of Schumann's *Symphonic Studies Op. 13* is dedicated to grace notes. I suggest treating and executing the groups of three grace notes like the triplet of thirty-second notes that Schumann does spell out. Thus, it is played on the fourth sixteenth of the beat, and when there is a note in the other hand on that fourth sixteenth of the beat, that note is played together with the first of the three grace notes. Measures 1-2:

In the *eleventh Etude* of the *Symphonic Studies* we find grace notes written for the RH on each of the beats in the third measure of the second ending. The grace notes leading to the third and fourth beats present fairly large leaps. I recommend playing each of the grace notes in this measure with the last thirty-second note of the previous beat in the LH, which plays quite fast, even though the tempo is *Andante*.

Breathing

We need to breathe, and so does music. Singers and wind players breathe automatically as they cannot physically sing or play if they don't breathe. Piano players tend to forget to breathe. It is best if we can relate our own breathing to the musical breathing. When we start to play the first note/chord of anything, whether a beginning of a piece or a beginning of a small phrase, we should do it while exhaling. Any long note/chord we play and hold should also be played and held while exhaling. When we slowly get off notes/chords, especially quiet ones and long ones like at various endings and pauses, we should inhale. How do we know when to get off a *fermata* note? A good indication would be when we run out of air. The time gap between the end of one phrase and the beginning of another, whether they are long or short phrases, definitely calls for a breath. Breathing can be better understood when it corresponds with the playing technique that uses vertical movements of the wrist. When the wrist sinks we breathe out and when the wrist elevates we breathe in. It is as if we had our lungs positioned under our wrists, and the wrists laying on the lungs. The wrists move down because we exhale and the lungs collapse. They move up because we inhale and the lungs inflate pushing the wrists upwards. We can practice this with rather long single notes/chords – what I call a one-note phrase. When we play the note/chord, the wrist moves downwards, and when we get off the note/chord the wrist moves upwards. We can also practice it with two-note phrases, though not very fast ones, or we will be panting like dogs. In two-note phrases we lower the wrist while exhaling when we play the first note of the phrase, and we elevate the wrist while inhaling when we play the second note of the phrase. For example, if we play in the RH D with finger 3 and C with finger 2 as a two-note phrase, we will exhale when playing finger 3 (wrist moves down),

and inhale when playing finger 2 (wrist moves up).

Playing Four Hands on One Piano

Two separate seats are preferred, as each seat can be individually set for the desired height and the desired distance from the piano. In order to help prevent the hands/arms of the two players from "clashing", the seating has to be with a slight angle towards the center of the keyboard as shown in the photo.

In order to help avoid hand/finger "collision" and possible injury, the players often have to play with the weak fingers of the hand that is close to the other player's hand. The *Secondo* cannot always afford to play with the most comfortable fingers in the RH, while the *Primo* cannot always afford to play with the most comfortable fingers in the LH.

For example: *Primo* has to play with the LH this beautiful ascending melody made of the notes middle C, D, and E. If it is a piano *solo*, we will naturally want to use our best/safest fingers, like 3-2-1, or perhaps 4-3-2. Since this is a duet, where *Secondo* has to play a long B (a step below the middle C) with the RH at the same time that *Primo* is playing C-D-E, *Primo* is forced to use the weak fingers and play C-D-E with 5-4-3. *Secondo* is also forced to use a weak finger, playing that long B with the little finger and not with any other comfortable/safe finger that could have been used in *solo* playing. This is shown in the following music example.

Crossing hands between the two players should be treated like crossing hands in *solo* playing: One player should play inward on the keys (toward the fall board) with a high wrist, while the other player should play outward on the keys (away from the fall board) and with a low wrist. The player who plays inward with the high wrist should try to avoid using the thumb, which, due to its shortness, may block the space underneath for the other player's hand to move about. The player who plays on more black keys will usually be the one playing or crossing on top, again, with a high wrist while inward on the keys. The player who plays on more white keys will usually be the one playing or crossing underneath, of course, with a low wrist while outward on the keys.

Sometimes redistribution of notes between the two players can also be very helpful. It can be anything from a single note to a whole passage. If the same note appears at the same time in both parts of the two players, one of the players should omit it.

The two players should breathe together as if they are one person. This will tremendously enhance the ensemble playing. Breathing together will help to start together without having to count the rhythm before starting. Breathing together will help to finish a piece, a movement, a section, or a phrase together, as well as to come off notes/chords together. Since breathing corresponds with hand movements and affects the produced sound, phrasing, and the playing in general, not only will breathing together enhance the beginnings and endings of pieces, phrases, etc., but it will also help create unified approaches towards these beginnings and endings and towards everything else within the musical piece.

Conclusion

It is my hope that I have covered in this book all piano-playing fingering issues, as well as some other inseparable areas of technique, exercises, breathing, phrasing, and various other musical concerns.

What I call advanced and innovative fingering comprises fingering ideas already used by Chopin, Liszt, and other virtuosos. I have to admit that almost nothing in this book is new. I hardly invented anything; almost everything was said and done before me. Things I say in this book are ideas and techniques that I learned from my teachers, learned from the music written by the great composers, read in books, picked up from other pianists, as well as arrived at by myself.

There are so many possible examples from the repertoire for most fingering issues that it was very hard to avoid the temptation of showing them all, and just keep them down to a few. However, the variety of examples often shows different angles of the same fingering issue. The reader is encouraged to find more examples for each and every fingering issue, as well as adopt the various recommendations and examine their suitability for any music.

Always remember this "key-note": comfort is good, efficiency is better. The first priority should be efficient fingering that serves the music and the health of your hands; only then comes comfortable fingering – whether it is for the mind or for the hands.

The pianist/reader can look for various fingering ideas according to the topics in the book, and can find them either by titles in the Contents or via the Index of names and terms. Here is a short summary regarding thoughts and actions in creating the best fingering solutions:

- The five-finger position and its expansions are the basis for all fingering ideas. One of the first things to do, therefore, is to check how much can be blocked into one hand position.
- We must remember, at the same time, the relationship between the topography of the keyboard with its groups of two and three black keys, and the anatomy of our hand with three long fingers and two short ones.
- Perhaps the next steps would be to check what needs to be worked out backwards and where to utilize finger crossing and thumb pivoting.
- It is always helpful to identify in the music: scales, chords, arpeggios, inversions, intervals, parallel or contrary motions, patterns, and sequences.

- It would be good, at this point, to solve problematic spots with the various fingering tools provided in the book.
- Everything, of course, should be done while paying attention to tempo, dynamics, accents, expression, phrasing, styles, etc., all of which can be influenced by fingering, or rather can influence one's fingering choices.

In general, it is recommended that you keep your mind and eyes wide open, and try to see the bigger picture. This often helps in creating good fingering while also helping the musical phrasing and interpretation. Look for what would best serve the music and you. Look for all the fingering possibilities and opportunities that the score offers and draw accordingly from the bank of all the suggested fingering tools in this book. Use your imagination, and don't hesitate to be creative and inventive.

I wish you – the pianist and reader of this book – much success in choosing fingering for the pieces you play. I hope that you enjoy using the book and that you derive endless pleasure and satisfaction from your own piano playing and music making.

Acknowledgments

I wish to thank from the bottom of my heart the people who helped me complete this book:

Albert Frantz, Andi Bar-Niv, David Lee, Jeremy Todd, Joseph De Alejandro, Lindy Mayfield, Margie Kohn, Michal and Uri Levite, Mimi Fachler, Nancy Burstein, Pnina Stern, Sheli Bar-Niv, Steve Chandler, Tal Bar-Niv, and Yair Barniv.

I apologize if I left out anyone.
RB

Many thanks to ACUM for their grant.

Index

abduction: 43
adduction: 43
Albéniz, *Asturias – Leyenda, Suite española*: 58
Alberti bass: 148
avant-garde: 10, 150

Bach, Anna Magdalena (A.M.B.): 147
  G major Minuet, BWV 114, Little Notebook: 48
  Musette, BWV 126, Little Notebook: 49
Bach, Carl Philipp Emanuel (C.P.E.): 7, 12
  Solfeggietto: 53
Bach, Johann Sebastian: 11, 12, 67, 68, 69, 103, 106, 112, 120, 129
  Italian Concerto, BWV 971: 57
  Prelude No. 1, Well Tempered Clavier, Book I: 44, 45, 46, 146
  Prelude No. 4, WTC, Book I: 103
  Prelude No. 5, WTC, Book I: 47
  Prelude No. 12, WTC, Book I: 104
  Toccata in C major, BWV 564 (Bach/Busoni): 113, 189, 190
Bar-Niv, Rami: 1, 6
  Breezy Rider Rag: 73
  Rhapsody in Blue and white: 150, 179, 180
Baroque: 146
Bartók, *Sonata*: 76, 82
basso buffo: 61
Beethoven: 12, 13, 103, 112, 116
  Concerto No. 1: 114, 115
  Concerto No. 3: 62, 116, 124
  Concerto No. 4: 85, 86, 98, 102, 111, 118, 154, 155, 156, 162, 163, 164, 165, 169
  Concerto No. 5: 51, 52, 169
  Sonata Op. 2, No. 3: 164
  Sonata Op. 10, No. 2: 147
  Sonata Op. 13, Pathétique: 13, 104
  Sonata Op. 31, No. 1: 62
  Sonata Op. 31, No. 2, Tempest: 69, 87
  Sonata Op. 49, No. 2: 83, 114, 115
  Sonata Op. 57, Appassionata: 91, 96, 134, 135
  Sonata Op. 109: 64, 65
  Sonata Op. 111: 104, 114

Brahms:
  Concerto No. 1: 158, 159, 165
  Concerto No. 2: 110, 158, 166, 167, 168, 169
  Paganini Variations, No. 7, Book I: 186
broken thirds: 61, 62
bunched fingers: 150, 151
Busoni: 113, 189, 190
butterfly technique: 95, 183

catching technique: 9, 183
center of the keyboard: 77, 143, 199
Chopin: 7, 8, 12, 33, 109, 112, 120, 201
  Ballade No. 1, Op. 23: 94, 149, 150
  Concerto No. 1: 158
  Étude Op. 10, No. 1: 59, 60
  Étude Op. 10, No. 2: 106
  Étude Op. 10, No. 3: 55, 56
  Étude Op. 10, No. 4: 67, 68
  Étude Op. 10, No. 5: 189
  Étude Op. 10, No. 7: 192
  Étude Op. 10, No. 8: 188, 189
  Étude Op. 10, No. 11: 188
  Étude Op. 10, No. 12: 111, 128, 133, 195, 196
  Étude Op. 25, No. 2: 98, 111
  Étude Op. 25, No. 6: 153
  Étude Op. 25, No. 8: 182
  Étude Op. 25, No. 10: 184, 185
  Fantasie Op. 49: 70
  Impromptu No. 1, Op. 29: 110
  Nocturne Op. 9, No. 2: 48, 72, 98
  Nocturne Op. 15, No. 1: 192
  Nocturne Op. 27, No. 2: 181
  Nocturne Op. 55, No. 1: 34
  Polonaise Fantaisie: 188
  Polonaise Op. 53: 103, 111, 126, 127
  Prelude Op. 28, No. 7: 74
  Prelude Op. 28, No. 16: 98, 99
  Prelude Op. 28, No. 24: 109, 184
  Scherzo No. 2, Op. 31: 69, 70, 192
  Scherzo No. 4, Op. 54: 193
  Sonata Op. 35: 57, 178, 179, 192, 193
  Sonata Op. 58: 148, 149, 177, 178

Waltz No. 14, Op. Posthumous: 99
Waltz Op. 34, No. 3: 191
Waltz Op. 69, No. 1: 121
Waltz Op. 69, No. 2: 34
chord shape: 37, 45
Clavierbüchlein: 147
Clementi: 12
contrary motion: 21, 43, 49, 50, 112, 122, 124, 125, 153, 162, 165, 201
Couperin, *Rondeau, Les Bergerie*s: 147
Czerny: 12

Debussy:
  Clair de Lune, Suite Bergamasque: 57, 58
  Jardins sous la pluie (*Gardens in the rain*): 138
  L'isle Joyeuse (*The Island of Pleasure*): 139
  Prelude No. 10, Book I, La Cathédrale engloutie (*The Sunken Cathedral*): 72, 73,
    74, 75
decay: 83, 146
diatonic intervals: 52, 53
distal: 103, 136, 140

eliminating notes: 167, 168, 169

fist: 10, 150

gaining extra finger: 67, 68, 86, 161
Gershwin:
  Concerto in F: 136, 137
  I Got Rhythm Variations, Chinese Variation: 141, 142
  Prelude No. 1: 59
  Prelude No. 2: 129, 130
  Rhapsody in Blue: 138, 187, 190, 191, 193, 194, 195
Grieg:
  Concerto: 156, 157, 158, 176
  Norwegian Dance No. 2: 127, 128
gruppetto: 97, 121

Handel, *Passacaglia, Suite No. 7*: 58
Hanon, *Exercise No. 1*: 52, 53
harmonic figuration: 130, 131
harmonic interval: 14, 32, 72, 82, 88, 90, 94, 96, 107, 136, 145

Haydn: 68
  D major Concerto: 97, 116, 117, 148
hidden patterns: 52, 53
Hummel: 12

injury/injury free: 6, 105, 110, 129, 144, 152, 199

jazz: 149
Joplin, *The Entertainer*: 34

karate chop: 81
Kullak: 12

Liszt: 8, 12, 109, 112, 120, 177, 201
  Concert Paraphrase on *Rigoletto* by Verdi: 95, 96, 101, 142
  Consolation No. 3: 130, 131
  Hungarian Rhapsody No. 11: 141
  Liebesträume No. 3: 131
  Mephisto Waltz: 64
  Transcendental Etude No. 4, Mazeppa: 82, 177

memory/memorizing/memorization/memorize: 7, 10, 44, 52, 55, 58, 167
Mendelssohn, *Rondo Capriccioso Op. 14*: 84, 85, 105,153
metacarpal joint: 81
mirroring image: 21, 37, 38, 122, 123
mode: 25, 26, 160, 161
  Dorian: 26
  Phrygian: 26
Mozart: 12, 61, 68, 112, 120, 129, 164
  Ah! vous dirai-je, Maman (Twinkle, Twinkle, Little Star): 68, 83, 86
  Concerto K. 488: 116, 117
  Rondo Alla Turca: 72, 97
  Sonata K. 279: 164
  Sonata K. 282: 63
  Sonata K. 283: 61
  Sonata K. 311: 146
  Sonata K. 331: 72, 97
  Sonata K. 332: 88, 117
  Sonata K. 333: 61
  Sonata K. 545: 115
  Sonata K. 576: 62, 63

nachschlag: 97, 98, 104, 164, 169

octatonic scale: 149
over-holding: 146
overlapping legato: 145
overtones: 10, 148

Paderewski, *Menuet à l'Antique Op. 14, No. 1*: 33
Paganini: 186
paired fingerings: 105
parallel fingering: 122, 125
parallel motion: 21, 112, 122, 124
pedal: 67, 68, 94, 102, 146, 147, 148, 149, 189, 191
    damper: 146
    sustain: 68, 84, 104, 106, 148
pentascale: 16, 122, 181
Petzold, Christian: 48
Piazzolla, *Invierno Porteño (Winter), The Four Seasons*: 180
pivotal fingering: 99
pivotal/pivoting thumb: 9, 11, 97, 98, 99, 116, 121, 201
pivoting finger: 99
prolonged touch: 146
pronation: 144
proximal: 136, 141

Rachmaninov: 8
    Concerto No. 2: 94
    Prelude Op. 3, No, 2: 54
    The Lilacs Op. 21, No. 5: 196
radial flexion: 43
Rameau: 12
Ravel
    Gaspard de la Nuit: 157, 195
    Sonatine: 139, 140
reciprocal fingering: 122, 124, 125
repetitive strain injury (RSI): 105, 152
rewrite/rewriting/rewritten: 75, 129, 130, 135, 159, 189, 190, 191
rotation: 9, 42, 99, 144
rule of thumb/no-thumb: 97, 140

Saint-Saëns, *Concerto No. 4*: 81, 82, 176
Scarlatti, Alessandro: 11
Scarlatti, Domenico: 11, 12
  Sonata K. 29 (L. 461, P. 85): 132, 140
Schubert
  Erlkönig: 95, 96, 135
  Impromptu Op. 90, No. 1: 181
  Impromptu Op. 90, No. 4: 34, 35
  Sonata Op. 143, D. 784: 197
Schumann: 8
  Papillons Op. 2: 184
  Symphonic Studies Op. 13: 197
Scriabin, *Etude Op. 8, No. 12*: 133
seventh (7th) chord/arpeggio: 33, 40, 41, 110, 119
slurred pairs: 61
strenuous: 33, 36, 59, 73, 75
stretch/stretching/stretched: 9, 33, 40, 50, 60, 71, 73, 75, 79, 84, 85, 110, 118, 119,
    129, 146, 150, 153, 156, 179, 180, 182, 190, 191
stretch free: 73, 118, 119
supination: 142

Tchaikovsky, *February (No. 2), The Seasons Op. 37a*: 55
tension/tension free: 9, 152
torso: 43
tremolo: 137, 155, 157, 158
Twinkle, Twinkle, Little Star: 68, 83, 86
two-note phrase: 61, 83, 87, 90, 198

ulnar flexion: 43

Verdi: 95
Villa-Lobos, *Preludio, Bachianas Brasileiras No. 4*: 56
vorschlag: 97

wrist circle: 35, 62

zigzag arpeggio: 50, 51, 131
zigzag scale: 61, 62

About the Author

Rami Bar-Niv is one of Israel's most acclaimed and sought after pianists. He travels extensively and has become an international citizen, concertizing all over the world. Born in Tel-Aviv in December 1945, Bar-Niv graduated with honors from the Rubin Academy of Music, and was the recipient of various prizes and scholarships. He won the America-Israel Cultural Foundation Competition and was awarded a scholarship to further his studies in the United States. After graduating from the Mannes College of Music in New York, where he studied with the renowned Mme. Nadia Reisenberg, he won numerous competitions, and embarked on a successful concert career. He is heard regularly in North, Central, and South America, Europe, Africa, Asia, Australia, New Zealand, and Israel, where he received the "Best Performer Award" from the Israeli government.

Rami Bar-Niv performs as a soloist with orchestras, as a recitalist, and as a chamber musician. He appears in live concerts, on radio, and on television, and is always received with great enthusiasm. Often sent abroad by the Foreign Ministry to represent Israel in concerts, he has become an ambassador of goodwill for Israel. Bar-Niv made history by being the first, and so far the only, Israeli artist to perform in Egypt following the Begin/Sadat Peace Treaty.

His recordings for CBS and other labels in Israel and abroad have met with praise and popularity. His compositions are published, recorded, and performed all over the world. He has often been at the top of the charts on various Internet music sites such as MP3.com, YouTube, and many others. Along with his concerts, he has been teaching all over the world, giving master classes, lectures, workshops, and private lessons. Since 2006 he has been offering a week-long piano camp for adults twice a year in the United States. He has published a number of articles in music magazines and has contributed thousands of posts on musical subjects to various Internet piano forums and groups. This is his first book.

Rami Bar-Niv lives in Raanana, Israel with his wife, Andi. They have two children: a son, Tal and a daughter, Sheli.

The New York Times wrote of Rami Bar-Niv: "Effective and Flamboyant"
The Boston Globe wrote of Rami Bar-Niv: "An original major talent"

http://www.ybarniv.com/Rami
http://www.youtube.com/user/barniv
http://ramisrhapsody.tripod.com/

Compositions by Rami Bar-Niv

3 Interludes for piano, AndreA 1041.
Blue-Rag for Brass Quintet, AndreA 1023.
Blue-Rag for piano, AndreA 1010.
Blue-Rag for trumpet/clarinet/flute/oboe/violin/viola/cello/alto-sax and piano,
AndreA 1012.
Breezy Rider Rag, Drag-Rag, and Blue-Rag for piano (simplified), AndreA 1015.
Breezy Rider Rag for piano, AndreA 1016.
Cadenza for Haydn, Piano Concerto in D major, 3rd movement, AndreA 1013.
Drag-Rag for piano, AndreA 1014.
Improvisation for cello solo, AndreA 1011B.
Improvisation for solo B-flat-trumpet/B-flat-clarinet, AndreA 1011C.
Improvisation for solo C-trumpet/violin/viola/flute/oboe, AndreA 1011/1011A.
Improvisation for trumpet/clarinet/flute/oboe/violin/viola/cello and piano,
AndreA 1022.
Israeli-Hassidic Songs for the Young Pianist, Or-Tav Music Publications.
Israeli Songs and Dances for the Young Pianist, Or-Tav Music Publications.
Israeli-Jewish Songs of Holidays for the Young Pianist, Or-Tav Music Publications.
Israeli Suite for string orchestra, AndreA 1042.
Longing For My Father, 7 songs without words for
trumpet/clarinet/flute/oboe/violin/viola/cello and piano, AndreA 1024C/1024B.
Longing For My Father, a cycle of 7 Holocaust songs for baritone and piano,
AndreA 1045.
Longing For My Father, a cycle of 7 Holocaust songs for soprano and orchestra,
AndreA 1044.
Longing For My Father, a cycle of 7 Holocaust songs for soprano and piano,
AndreA 1024.
Plain Ol' Rag for piano, AndreA 1019.
Plain Ol' Rag for piano 4 hands, AndreA 1020.
Pokarekare Variations for piano, AndreA 1046.
Prayer and Dance for 2 pianos, AndreA 1048.
Prayer and Dance for piano, Israeli Music Publication, IMP 295.
Prayer for Organ, AndreA 1047.
Rhapsody in Blue and White for piano, AndreA 1021.
Sephardic Melody (Paul Ben-Haim) arr. for piano, IMP 125/p.
Shmateh-Rag for piano (simplified), AndreA 1029.
Shmateh-Rag for piano, AndreA 1028.
Shmateh-Rag for piano 4 hands, AndreA 1030.
Shmateh-Rag for trumpet/clarinet/flute/oboe/violin/viola/cello/alto-sax and piano,
AndreA 1040.

Toccata for orchestra, or 11 instruments and percussion, AndreA.
Toccata for piano, Israel Music Institute, IMI 6348.
Toccata for trumpet and piano, AndreA 1043.
Vocalise (Etude, on J. S. Bach, Prelude in C) for piano, AndreA 1026.
Vocalise (on J. S. Bach, Prelude in C) for piano 4 hands, AndreA 1027.
Vocalise (on J. S. Bach, Prelude in C) for
        trumpet/clarinet/flute/oboe/violin/viola/cello/alto-sax and piano, AndreA 1025.

Also on AndreA

Abraham Kolam – Toccatina for piano, AndreA 1018.
Sheli Bar-Niv – Opus 1 for piano, AndreA 1017.
Sheli Bar-Niv/Rami Bar-Niv – Opus 1 for two clarinets, AndreA 1017B.
William Gunther-Sprecher – Jerusalem Concerto for piano.

New (2012)

Rami Bar-Niv – Jazzkid for piano, 14 short jazz pieces that range from mid-elementary to intermediate in a progressing order, AndreA 1049.

New (2013)

Rami Bar-Niv – Traditional Hebrew Songs for piano, late Elementary and Intermediate, AndreA 1050.

Endorsements

Dr. Walden Hughes, Professor of Piano, Northwest Nazarene University

"The Art of Piano Fingering: Traditional, Advanced, and Innovative" by Rami Bar-Niv, fills a tremendous void in the realm of the pianistic world. Published in 2012, it is the first book of its kind in the 303 year history of the piano. Mr. Bar-Niv, a world-renowned concert artist and master teacher, who hails from his native Israel and has performed extensively on 5 continents, has recognized that although virtuoso pianists have learned to categorize patterns and figure out the best fingerings as they learn new repertoire, no one has systematized the process over the past 3 centuries in a way that can be taught effectively to others.

Students are typically simply left to flounder as they wallow and stumble through learning new pieces, with only the standard scale and arpeggio fingerings to guide them. Although scales and arpeggios are a helpful part of the process to understanding keyboard topography, how much of the fingering selection process for the piano repertoire is solved simply by knowing your scales and arpeggios?

Glancing at the Table of Contents, prior to reading this outstanding book, I became very excited and recognized immediately the remarkable contribution Mr. Bar-Niv has made to pianistic society world-wide. Only Carl Philipp Emanuel Bach's Essay on the True Art of Playing Keyboard Instruments comes anywhere near this effort, and although it had a great impact on 18th century keyboard players, that treatise was conceived and written for harpsichordists, not pianists.

"The Art of Piano Fingering" is an exceptional contribution to the future of pianism, and should be required reading for all piano teachers and piano students. Order your copy today; you will be immensely grateful you did!

Jeremy Todd, an adult piano student and main contributor to the book editing

This book is the first of its kind, and it is perhaps three hundred years overdue. The subject matter is important for pianists of all skill levels, and the depth of coverage will surprise even the most accomplished pianists. Central to the book are a few simple and powerful ideas, which naturally lead to an extensive set of guidelines for handling any fingering challenge. For those new to the art of fingering, the book contains interesting background material as well as plenty of practical advice about each new idea. For the more advanced audience, the book is also a complete reference for fingering tools and strategies. All readers, no matter how advanced, are certain to find novel and useful approaches to fingering here. Countless examples from well-known scores, as well as photographs of the actual techniques in use, make the book very clear and easy to follow. Given how important and powerful well-chosen fingering can be, this book is essential for any serious student of the piano.

Made in the USA
Middletown, DE
06 February 2018